Sharing Big Data Safely
Managing Data Security

Ted Dunning and Ellen Friedman

Beijing · Boston · Farnham · Sebastopol · Tokyo

Sharing Big Data Safely

Ted Dunning and Ellen Friedman

Published by O'Reilly Media, Inc., 1005 Gravenstein Highway North, Sebastopol, CA 95472.

O'Reilly books may be purchased for educational, business, or sales promotional use. Online editions are also available for most titles (*http://safaribooksonline.com*). For more information, contact our corporate/institutional sales department: 800-998-9938 or corporate@oreilly.com .

Editors: Holly Bauer and Tim McGovern   **Cover Designer:** Randy Comer

September 2015:   First Edition

Revision History for the First Edition
2015-09-02:   First Release
2015-12-11:   Second Release

978-1-491-95212-2

[LSI]

Table of Contents

Preface

This is not a book to tell you how to build a security system. It's not about how to lock data down. Instead, we provide solutions for how to share secure data safely.

The benefit of collecting large amounts of many different types of data is now widely understood, and it's increasingly important to keep certain types of data locked down securely in order to protect it against intrusion, leaks, or unauthorized eyes. Big data security techniques are becoming very sophisticated. But how do you keep data secure and yet get access to it when needed, both for people within your organization and for outside experts? The challenge of balancing security with safe sharing of data is the topic of this book.

These suggestions for safely sharing data fall into two groups:

- How to share original data in a controlled way such that each different group using it—such as within your organization—only sees part of the whole dataset.
- How to employ synthetic data to let you get help from outside experts without ever showing them original data.

The book explains in a non-technical way how specific techniques for safe data sharing work. The book also reports on real-world use cases in which customized synthetic data has provided an effective solution. You can read Chapters 1–4 and get a complete sense of the story.

In Chapters 5–7, we go on to provide a technical deep-dive into these techniques and use cases and include links to open source code and tips for implementation.

Who Should Use This Book

If you work with sensitive data, personally identifiable information (PII), data of great value to your company, or any data for which you've made promises about disclosure, or if you consult for people with secure data, this book should be of interest to you. The book is intended for a mixed non-technical and technical audience that includes decision makers, group leaders, developers, and data scientists.

Our starting assumption is that you know how to build a secure system and have already done so. The question is: do you know how to safely share data without losing that security?

CHAPTER 1
So Secure It's Lost

What do buried 17th-century treasure, encoded messages from the Siege of Vicksburg in the US Civil War, tree squirrels, and big data have in common?

Someone buried a massive cache of gemstones, coins, jewelry, and ornate objects under the floor of a cellar in the City of London, and it remained undiscovered and undisturbed there for about 300 years. The date of the burying of this treasure is fixed with considerable confidence over a fairly narrow range of time, between 1640 and 1666. The latter was the year of the Great Fire of London, and the treasure appeared to have been buried before that destructive event. The reason to conclude that the cache was buried after 1640 is the presence of a small, chipped, red intaglio with the emblem of the newly appointed 1st Viscount Stafford, an aristocratic title that had only just been established that year. Many of the contents of the cache appear to be from approximately that time period, late in the time of Shakespeare and Queen Elizabeth I. Others—such as a cameo carving from Egypt—were probably already quite ancient when the owner buried the collection of treasure in the early 17th century.

What this treasure represents and the reason for hiding it in the ground in the heart of the City of London are much less certain than its age. The items were of great value even at the time they were hidden (and are of much greater value today). The location where the treasure was buried was beneath a cellar at what was then 30–32 Cheapside. This spot was in a street of goldsmiths, silversmiths, and other jewelers. Because the collection contains a combination of set and unset jewels and because the location of the hiding place was under a building owned at the time by the Goldsmiths' Company, the most likely explanation is that it was the stock-in-trade of a jeweler operating at that location in London in the early 1600s.

Why did the owner hide it? The owner may have buried it as a part of his normal work—as perhaps many of his fellow jewelers may have done from time to time with their own stock—in order to keep it secure during the regular course of business. In other words, the hidden location may have been functioning as a very inconvenient, primitive safe when something happened to the owner.

Most likely the security that the owner sought by burying his stock was in response to something unusual, a necessity that arose from upheavals such as civil war, plague, or an elevated level of activity by thieves. Perhaps the owner was going to be away for an extended time, and he buried the collection of jewelry to keep it safe for his return. Even if the owner left in order to escape the Great Fire, it's unlikely that that conflagration prevented him from returning to recover the treasure. Very few people died in the fire. In any event, something went wrong with the plan. One assumes that if the location of the valuables were known, someone would have claimed it.

Another possible but less likely explanation is that the hidden bunch of valuables were stolen goods, held by a fence who was looking for a buyer. Or these precious items might have been secreted away and hoarded up a few at a time by someone employed by (and stealing from) the jeweler or someone hiding stock to obscure shady dealings, or evade paying off a debt or taxes. That idea isn't so far-fetched. The collection is known to contain two counterfeit balas rubies that are believed to have been made by the jeweler Thomas Sympson of Cheapside. By 1610, Sympson had already been investigated for alleged fraudulent activities. These counterfeit stones are composed of egg-shaped quartz treated to accept a reddish dye, making them look like a type of large and very valuable ruby that was highly desired at the time. Regardless of the reason the treasure was hidden, something apparently went wrong for it to have remained undiscovered for so many years.

Although the identity of the original owner and his particular reasons for burying the collection of valuables may remain a mystery, the surprising story of the treasure's recovery is better known. Excavations for building renovations at that address were underway in 1912 when workers first discovered pieces of treasure, and soon the massive hoard was unearthed underneath a cellar. These workers sold pieces mainly to a man nicknamed "Stony Jack" Lawrence, who in turn sold this treasure trove to several London museums. It is fairly astounding that this now-famous Cheapside Hoard thus made its way into preservation in museum collections rather than entirely disappearing among the men who found it. It is also surprising that apparently no attempt was made for the treasure (or for compensation) to go to the owners of the land who had authorized the excavation, the Goldsmiths' Company.[1]

Today the majority of the hoard is held by the Museum of London (*http://bit.ly/1i1IjO1*), where it has been previously put on public display. A few other pieces of the treasure reside with the British Museum and the Victoria and Albert Museum. The Museum of London collection comprises spectacular pieces, including the light-hearted emerald salamander pictured in Figure 1-1.

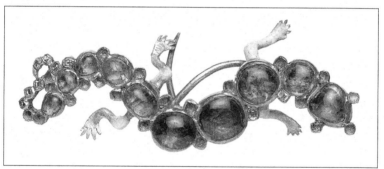

Figure 1-1. Emerald salamander hat ornament from the Cheapside Hoard, much of which is housed in the Museum of London. This elaborate and whimsical piece of jewelry reflects the international nature of the jewelry business in London in the 17th century when the collection was hidden, presumably for security. The emeralds came from Colombia, the diamonds likely from India, and the gold work is European in style. (Image credit: Museum of London, image ID 65634, used with permission.)

---

1 Fosyth, Hazel. *Cheapside Hoard: London's Lost Treasures: The Cheapside Hoard (http:// bit.ly/cheapside-hoard-bk).* London: Philip Wilson Publishers, 2013.

Salamanders were sometimes used as symbol of renewal because they were believed to be able to emerge unharmed from a fire. This symbol seems appropriate for an item that survived the Great Fire of London as well as 300 years of being hidden. It was so well hidden, in fact, that with the rest of the hoard, it was lost even to the heirs of the original owner. *This lost treasure was a security failure.*

It was as important then as it is now to keep valuables in a secure place, otherwise they would likely disappear at the hands of thieves. But in the case of the Cheapside Hoard, the security plan went awry. Although the articles were of great value, no one related to the original owner claimed them throughout the centuries. Regardless of the exact identity of the original owner who hid the treasure, this story illustrates a basic challenge: there is a tension between locking down things of value to keep them secure and doing so in a way that they can be accessed and used appropriately and safely. The next story shows a different version of the problem.

During the American Civil War in the 1860s, both sides made use of several different cipher systems to encode secret messages. The need to guard information about troop movements, supplies, strategies, and the whereabouts of key officers or political figures is obvious, so encryption was a good idea. However, some of the easier codes were broken, while others posed a different problem. The widely employed Vigenére cipher (*http://bit.ly/1gXTHJG*), for example, was so difficult to use for encryption or for deciphering messages that mistakes were often made. A further problem that arose because the cipher was hard to use correctly was that comprehension of an important message was sometimes perilously delayed.[2] The Vigenére cipher table is shown in Figure 1-2.

---

2 Civil War Code (*http://nyti.ms/1Jy3Bx1*)

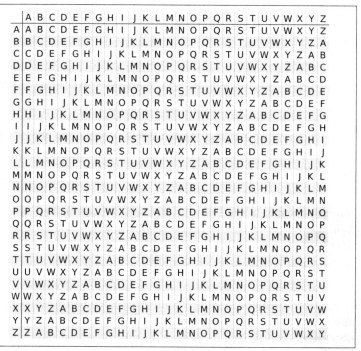

Figure 1-2. The Vigenére square used to encode and decipher messages. While challenging to break, this manual encryption system was reported to be very difficult to use accurately and in a timely manner. (Image by Brandon T. Fields. Public domain via Wikimedia Commons (http://bit.ly/1TTZ61f).)

One such problem occurred during the Vicksburg Campaign. A Confederate officer, General Johnson, sent a coded message to General Kirby requesting troop reinforcements. Johnson made errors in encrypting the message using the difficult Vigenére cipher. As a result, Kirby spent 12 hours trying to decode the message—unsuccessfully. He finally resorted to sending an officer back to Johnson to get a direct message. The delay was too long; no help could be sent in time. A strong security method had been needed to prevent the enemy from reading messages, but the security system also needed to allow reasonably functional and timely use by both the sender and the intended recipient.

This Civil War example, like the hidden and lost Cheapside treasure, illustrates the idea that *sometimes the problem with security is not a leak but a lock.* Keeping valuables or valuable information safe is important, but it must be managed in such a way that it does not lock out the intended user.

In modern times, this delicate balance between security and safe access is a widespread issue. Even individuals face this problem almost daily. Most people are sufficiently savvy to avoid using an obvious or easy-to-remember password such as a birthday, pet name, or company name for access to secure online sites or to access a bank account via a cash point machine or ATM. But the problem with a not-easy-to-remember password is that it's not easy to remember!

This situation is rather similar to what happens when tree squirrels busily hide nuts in the lawn, presumably to protect their hoard of food. Often the squirrels forget where they've put the nuts—you may have seen them digging frantically trying to find a treasure—with the result of many newly sprouted saplings the next year.

In the trade-off of problems related to security and passwords, it's likely more common to forget your password than to undergo an attack, but that doesn't mean it's a good idea to forego using an obscure password. For the relatively simple situation of passwords, people (unlike tree squirrels) can of course get help. There are password-management systems to help people handle their obscure passwords. Of course these systems must themselves be carefully designed in order to remain secure.

These examples all highlight the importance of protecting something of value, even valuable data, but avoiding the problem that it becomes "so secure it's lost."

Safe Access in Secure Big Data Systems

Our presumption is that you've probably read about 50 books on locking down data. But the issue we're tackling in this book is quite a different sort of problem: how to safely access or share data after it is secured.

As we begin to see the huge benefits of saving a wide range of data from many sources, including system log files, sensor data, user behavior histories, and more, big data is becoming a standard part of our lives. Of course many types of big data need to be protected through strong security measures, particularly if it involves personally identifiable information (PII), government secrets, or the like.

The sectors that first come to mind when considering who has serious requirements for security are the financial, insurance, and health care sectors and government agencies. But even retail merchants or online services have PII related to customer accounts. The need for tight security measures is therefore widespread in big data systems, involving standard security processes such as authentication, authorization, encryption, and auditing. Emerging big data technologies, including Hadoop- and NoSQL-based platforms, are being equipped with these capabilities, some through integrated features and others through add-on features or via external tools. In short, secured big data systems are widespread.

For the purposes of this book, we assume as our starting point that you've already got your data locked down securely.

Locking down sensitive data (or hiding valuables) well such that thieves cannot reach it makes sense, but of course you also need to be able to get access when desired, and that in turn can create vulnerability. Consider this analogy: if you want to keep an intruder from entering a door, the safest bet is to weld the door shut. Of course, doing so makes the door almost impossible to use—that's why people generally use padlocks instead of welding. But the fact is, as soon as you give out the combination or key to the padlock, you've slightly increased the risk of an unwanted intruder getting entry. Sharing a way to unlock the door to important data is a necessary part of using what you have, but you want to do so carefully, and in ways that will minimize the risk.

So with that thought, we begin our look at what happens when you need to access or share secure data. Doing this safely is not always as easy as it sounds, as shown by the examples we discuss in the next chapter. Then, in Chapter 3 and Chapter 4, we introduce two different solutions to the problem that enable you to safely manage how you use secure data. We also describe some real-world success stories that have already put these ideas into practice. These descriptions, which are non-technical, show you how these approaches work and the basic idea of how you might put them to use in your own situations. The remaining chapters provide a technical deep-dive into the implementation of these techniques, including a link to open source code that should prove helpful.

CHAPTER 2

The Challenge: Sharing Data Safely

Sharing data safely isn't a simple thing to do.

In order for well-protected data to be of use, you have to be able to manage safe access within your organization or even make it possible for others outside your group to work with secure data. People focus a lot of attention on how to protect their system from intrusion by an attacker, and that is of course a very important thing to get right. But it's a different matter to consider how to maintain security when you intentionally share data. How can you do that safely? That is the question we examine in this book.

People recognize the value and potential in collecting and persisting large amounts of data in many different situations. This big data is not just archived—it needs to be readily available to be analyzed for many purposes, from business reporting, targeted marketing campaigns, and discovering financial trends to situations that can even save lives. For instance, machine learning techniques can take advantage of the powerful combination of long-term, detailed maintenance histories for parts and equipment in big industrial settings, along with huge amounts of time series sensor data, in order to discover potential problems before they cause catastrophic damage and possibly even cost lives. This ability to do predictive maintenance is just one of many ways that big data keeps us safe. Detection of threatening activities, including terrorism or fraud attacks, relies on having enough data to be able to recognize what normal behavior looks like so that you can build effective ways to discover anomalies.

Big data, like all things of value, needs to be handled carefully in order to be secure. In this book we look at some simple but very effective ways to do this when data is being accessed, shared, and used. Before we discuss those approaches, however, we first take a look at some of the problems that can arise when secure data is shared, depending on how that is done.

Surprising Outcomes with Anonymity

One of the most challenging and extreme cases of managing secure data is to make a sensitive dataset publicly available. There can be huge benefits to providing public access to large datasets of interesting information, such as promoting the greater understanding of social or physical trends or by encouraging experimentation and innovation through new analytic and machine learning techniques. Data of public interest includes collections such as user behavior histories involving patterns of music or movie engagement, purchases, queries, or other transactions. Access to real data not only inspires technological advances, it also provides realistic and consistent ways to test performance of existing systems and tools.

To the causal observer, it may seem obvious that the safe way to share data publicly while protecting privacy is to cleanse the data of sensitive information—such as so-called *micro-data* that contains information specific to an individual—before sharing. The goal is to provide anonymity when releasing a dataset publicly and therefore to make the data available for analysis without compromising the users' privacy. However, truly unreversible anonymity is actually very difficult to achieve.

Protecting privacy in publicly available datasets is a challenge, although the issues and pitfalls are becoming clearer as we all gain experience. Some people or organizations, of course, are just careless or naïve when handling or sharing sensitive data, so problems ensue. This is especially an issue with very large datasets because they carry their own (and new) types of risk if not managed properly. But even expert and experienced data handlers who take privacy seriously and who are trying to be responsible face a challenge when making data public. This was especially true in the early days of big data, before certain types of risk were fully recognized. That's what happened with a famous case of data shared for a big data machine learning competition conceived by Netflix, a leading online streaming and DVD video subscription service company and a big data technology leader. Although the contest was successful, there were unexpected side effects of sharing anonymized data, as you will see.

The Netflix Prize

On October 2, 2006, Netflix initiated a data mining contest with these words:

"We're quite curious, really. To the tune of one million dollars."[1]

The goal of the contest was to substantially improve the movie recommendation system already in practice at Netflix. The data to be used was released to all who registered for the contest and was in the form of movie ratings and their dates that had been made by a subset of Netflix subscribers prior to 2005. The prize was considerable, as was the worldwide reaction to the contest: over 40,000 teams from 186 countries registered to participate. There would be progress prizes each year plus the grand prize of one million dollars. The contest was set to run potentially for five years. This was a big deal.

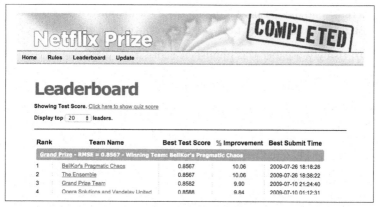

Figure 2-1. Screenshot of the Netflix Prize website showing the final leading entries. Note that the second place entry got the same score as the winning entry but was submitted just 20 minutes later than the

---

1 http://www.netflixprize.com/rules.

one that took the $1,000,000 prize. From http://www.netflixprize.com/
leaderboard.

Unexpected Results from the Netflix Contest

Now for the important part, in so far as our story is concerned. The dataset that was made public to participants in the contest consisted of 100,480,507 movie ratings from 480,189 subscribers from December 1999 to December 2005. This data was a subset drawn from ratings by the roughly 4 million subscribers Netflix had by the end of the time period in question. The contest data was about 1/8 of the total data for ratings.

In order to protect the privacy and personal identification of the Netflix subscribers whose data was being released publicly, Netflix provided anonymity. They took privacy seriously, as reflected in this response to a question on an FAQ posted at the Netflix Prize website:

> Q: "Is there any customer information that should be kept private?"
>
> A: "No, all customer identifying information has been removed. All that remains are ratings and dates..."

The dataset that was published for the contest appeared to be sufficiently stripped of personally identifying information (PII) so that there was no danger in making it public for the purposes of the contest. But what happened next was counterintuitive.

Surprisingly, a paper was published February 5, 2008 that explained how the anonymity of the Netflix contest data could be broken. The paper was titled "Robust De-anonymization of Large Datasets (How to Break Anonymity of the Netflix Prize Dataset)."[2] In it the authors, Arvind Narayana, now at Princeton, and Vitaly Shmatikov, now at University of Texas, Austin, explained a method for de-anonymizing data that applied to the Netflix example and more.

While the algorithms these privacy experts put forth are fairly complicated and technical, the idea underlying their approach is relatively simple and potentially widely applicable. The idea is this: when people anonymize a dataset, they strip off or encrypt information that could personally identify specific individuals. This infor-

---

2 http://arxiv.org/pdf/cs/0610105v2.pdf

mation generally includes things such as name, address, Social Security number, bank account number, or credit card number. It would seem there is no need to worry about privacy issues if this data is cleansed before it's made public, but that's not always true.

The problem lies in the fact that while the anonymized dataset alone may be relatively safe, it does not exist in a vacuum. It may be that other datasets could be used as a reference to supply background information about the people whose data is included in the anonymous dataset. When background information from the reference dataset is compared to or combined with the anonymized data and analyses are carried out, it may be possible to break the anonymity of the test set in order to reveal the identity of specific individuals whose data is included. The result is that, although the original PII has been removed from the published dataset, privacy is no longer protected. The basis for this de-anonymization method is depicted diagrammatically in Figure 2-2.

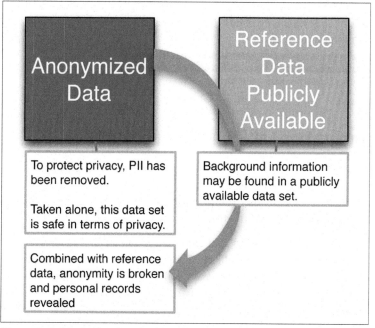

Figure 2-2. Method to break anonymity in a dataset using cross-correlation to other publicly available data. For the Netflix Prize example, Narayana and Shmatikov used a similar method. Their background information (dataset shown on the right here) was movie rating and date data from the Internet Movie Database (IMDB) that

was used to unravel identities and ratings records of subscribers whose data was included in the anonymized Netflix contest dataset.

Narayana and Smatikov experimented with the contest data for the Netflix Prize to see if it could be de-anonymized by this method. As a reference dataset, they used the publically available IMDB data. The startling observation was that an adversary trying to reveal identities of subscribers along with their ratings history only needed to know a small amount of auxiliary information, and that reference information did not even have to be entirely accurate. These authors showed that their method worked well with sparse datasets such as those commonly found for individual transactions and preferences. For the Netflix Prize example, they used this approach to achieve the results presented in Table 2-1.

Table 2-1. An adversary needs very little background cross-reference information to break anonymity of a dataset and reveal the identity of records for a specific individual. The results shown in this table reflect the level of information needed to de-anonymize the Netflix Prize dataset of movie ratings and dates.

Number of movie ratings	Error for date	Identities revealed
8 ratings (2 could be wrong)	± 14 days	99%
2 ratings	±3 days	68%

Implications of Breaking Anonymity

While it is surprising that the anonymity of the movie ratings dataset could be broken with so little auxiliary information, it may appear to be relatively unimportant—after all, they are only movie ratings. Why does this matter?

It's a reasonable question, but the answer is that it does matter, for several reasons. First of all, even with movie ratings, there can be serious consequences. By revealing the movie preferences of individuals, there can be implications of apparent political preferences, sexual orientation, or other sensitive personal information. Perhaps more importantly, the question in this particular case is not whether or not the average subscriber was worried about exposure of his or her movie preferences but rather whether or not any subscriber is concerned that his or her privacy was potentially compromised.[3] Additionally, the pattern of exposing identities in data that was thought to be anonymized applies to other types of datasets, not just to movie ratings. This issue potentially has widespread implications.

Taken to an extreme, problems with anonymity could be a possible threat to future privacy. Exposure of personally identifiable information not only affects privacy in the present, but it can also affect how much is revealed about you in the future. Today's de-anonymized dataset, for instance, could serve as the reference data for background information to be cross-correlated with future anonymized data in order to reveal identities and sensitive information recorded in the future.

Even if the approach chosen is to get permission from individuals before their data is made public, it's still important to make certain that this is done with fully informed consent. People need to realize that this data might be used to cross-reference other, similar datasets and be aware of the implications.

In summary, the Netflix Prize event was successful in many ways. It inspired more experimentation with data mining at scale, and it further established the company's reputation as a leader in working with large-scale data. Netflix was not only a big data pioneer with regard to data mining, but their contest also inadvertently raised awareness about the care that is needed when making sensitive data public. The first step in managing data safely is to be fully aware of where potential vulnerabilities lie. Forewarned is forearmed, as the saying goes.

Be Alert to the Possibility of Cross-Reference Datasets

The method of cross-correlation to reveal what is hidden in data can be a risk in many different settings. A very simple but relatively serious example is shown by the behavior reported for two parking garages that were located near one another in Luxembourg. Both garages allowed payment by plastic card (i.e., debit, credit). On the receipts that each vendor provided to the customer, part of the card

---

3 *Ibid.*

number was obscured in order to protect the account holder. Figure 2-3 illustrates how this was done, and why it posed a security problem.

Figure 2-3. The importance of protecting against unwanted cross-correlation. The fictitious credit card receipts depicted here show a pattern of behavior by two different parking vendors located in close proximity. Each one employs a similar system to obscure part of the PAN (primary account number) such that someone seeing the receipt will not get access to the account. Each taken alone is fairly secure. But what happens when the same customer has used both parking garages and someone gets access to both receipts?[4]

This problem with non-standard ways to obscure credit card numbers is one that could and should certainly be avoided. The danger becomes obvious when both receipts are viewed together. What we have here is a correlation attack in miniature. Once again, each dataset (receipt) taken alone may be secure, but when they are combined, information intended to stay obscured can be revealed. This time, however, the situation isn't complicated or even subtle. The solution is easy: use a standard approach to obscuring the card

4 http://bit.ly/card-digits

numbers, such as always revealing only the last four digits. Being aware of the potential risk and exercising reasonable caution should prevent problems like this.

New York Taxicabs: Threats to Privacy

Although the difficulties that can arise from trying to produce anonymity to protect privacy have now been well publicized, problems continue to occur, especially when anonymization is attempted by people inexperienced with managing privacy and security. They may make naïve errors because they underestimate the care that is needed, or they lack the knowledge of how to execute protective messages correctly.

An example of an avoidable error can be found in the 2014 release of detailed trip data for taxi cab drivers in New York City. This data was released in response to a public records request. The data included fare logs and historical information about trips, including pick-up and drop-off information. Presumably in order to protect the privacy of the drivers, the city made efforts to obscure medallion numbers and hack license numbers in the data. (Medallion numbers are assigned to yellow cabs in NYC; there are a limited number of them. Hack licenses are the driver's licenses needed to drive a medallion cab.)

The effort to anonymize the data was done via one-way cryptographic hashes for the hack license number and for the medallion numbers. These one-way hashes prevent a simple mathematical conversion of the encrypted numbers back to the original versions. Sounds good in theory, but (paraphrasing Einstein) theory and practice are the same, in theory only. The assumed protection offered by the anonymization methods used for the New York taxi cab data took engineer Vijay Pandurangan just two hours to break during a developers boot camp. Figure 2-4 provides a reminder of this problem.

Figure 2-4. Publicly released trip data for New York taxi cabs was de-anonymized in just hours during a hackathon in 2014, revealing the identity of individual drivers along with the locations and times of their trips.

Pandurangan noticed a serious weakness in the way the hack and medallion numbers had been obscured. Because each of the license systems has a predictable pattern, it was easy for him to construct a pre-computed table of all possible values and use it to de-anonymize the data.[5] This problem might have been avoided by executing the hash differently: if a random number had first been added to each identifier and then the hash carried out, anonymity could have been maintained. This well-known approach is called "salting the data."

Why does the lack of privacy protection matter for taxi data? Adversaries could calculate the gross income of the driver or possibly draw conclusions about where he or she is likely to live. Alternatively, a photo might show a passenger entering or exiting a cab along with the medallion number. This information could be correlated with the medallion numbers and trip records if the published data is not correctly de-anonymized. Once again, however, the point is not the

---

5 Goodin, Dan. "Poorly anonymized logs reveal NYC cab driver's detailed whereabouts." *Ars Technica*, 23 June 2014 (http://bit.ly/nyc-taxi-data).

specific method of de-anonymization, but rather that privacy was attempted and broken because protection was not done with sufficient care.

We relate stories such as these just as a reminder to take the task of sharing data seriously. The point here is to recognize the value in maintaining large datasets but also to protect them through careful and effective management of shared data. If sensitive data is to be published, adequate precautions should be taken and possibly expert advice should be consulted.

Sharing Data Safely

This book is about the flip side of data security: how to safely access and use data that is securely locked down. Now that we've taken a good look at some of the challenges faced when data is shared, you'll be aware of why carefully managed access is important.

The good news is that in this book we offer some practical and effective solutions that let you safely make use of data in secure environments. In Chapter 3, we present a convenient and reliable way to provide safe access to original data on a need-to-know basis. This approach is particularly useful for different groups within your own organization.

Sometimes you want to share data with outsiders. This might be in order to make a dataset publicly available or so that you can consult outside experts. Out of caution or even due to legal restrictions, you may not be able to show data directly to outsiders. For these situations, we provide a method of generating synthetic data using open source software known as log-synth such that the outsiders never actually see real data (a particularly safe approach). We introduce this method in Chapter 4 along with real-world examples that show how it has been put into use. In subsequent chapters, we provide technical details for these use cases as well as for general implementation.

CHAPTER 3

Data on a Need-to-Know Basis

Let's go back to buried treasure for a moment, to the exciting idea of a treasure map. Making a map avoids the problem suffered by the lost Cheapside Hoard described in Chapter 1. With a map, there's a way to get access to what is valuable even if something happens to the owner; the knowledge is not lost with the disappearance of that one person. But if a team is involved with hunting for the treasure, likely you'd want to be cautious and have a way to insure cooperation among the members. What do you do?

One trick is to cut the treasure map into pieces and give only one piece to each person involved in the hunt in order to essentially encrypt the map (in so far as any one person is concerned). That way, while each individual works with the real clues, each person knows only a part of the whole story, as demonstrated in Figure 3-1. This approach not only provides an enticing plot line for tales of adventure, it also has implications for big data and security.

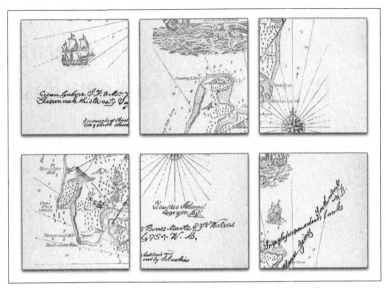

Figure 3-1. Pieces of the famous treasure map from the 19th-century fictitious adventure story Treasure Island by Robert Louis Stevenson, shown here out of order. Each piece of a treasure map provides only a partial view of the information about where treasure can be found. Imagine if you had only one of these pieces how much harder the task would be than if you had gotten the entire map.[1]

The idea of having only a piece or two pieces of a treasure map is analogous to a useful technique for safely sharing original data within a select group: a person or group who needs access to sensitive data gets to see original data, but only on a need-to-know basis. You provide permissions specifically restricted to the part of a dataset that is needed; the user does not see the entire story.

Views: A Secure Way to Limit What Is Seen

How can this partial sharing of data be done conveniently, safely, and in a fine-grained way for large-scale data? One way is to take advantage of an open source big data tool known as Apache Drill, which enables you to conveniently make views of data that limit what each user can "see" or access, as we will explain later in this chapter. People who are familiar with standard SQL will likely also

---

1 Image in public domain via Wikimedia commons (*http://bit.ly/1huI90R*).

be familiar with the concept of views. A view is a query that can be named and stored. You can design the view such that it allows the user to whom you give permissions to access only selected parts of the original data source. This control over permissions makes it possible for you to manage which users see which data, as depicted in Figure 3-2.

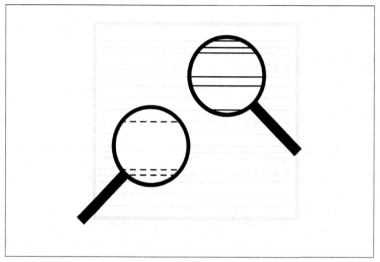

Figure 3-2. You can use views to provide a different view of data for different users. Each user who has permission for the view sees only the data specified in the view; the remainder of data in the table is invisible to them.

The view becomes the "world as they know it" to the user; you keep the full dataset private. The user can design different queries against the view just as they would do for a table. As data is updated in the table, the user sees the updated information if it is addressed by the view to which they have permission. Views don't take up space; they are not a sub-copy of data, so they don't consume additional space on disk. Views can be useful for a variety of reasons, including managing secure access, simplifying access to aggregated data, and providing a less-complex view of data to make certain types of analysis easier.

Although views are not a new concept, they are sometimes overlooked, particularly in the case of providing security, unless a person is very experienced with standard SQL. This is particularly true in the Hadoop and NoSQL environment, where the support for views with SQL-like tools has been uneven, particularly with respect to permissions. You may be surprised to know that the relatively new Apache Drill tool is different: it makes it convenient to create SQL views with permission chaining in the Hadoop or NoSQL big data space.

Before we tell you more about Apache Drill and how to use it to create views that help you manage data sharing, let's first explore some of the situations that motivate this security technique.

Why Limit Access?

The idea of providing different people or groups with different levels of detail in data is widespread. Think of the simple situation in which a charity publishes reports of who has donated and at what level. These reports are made public to show appreciation to donors as well as to inspire others to make a gift. Typically a report like this is a list with the donor's name assigned to categories for how much was given. These categories are often named, such as "silver, gold, platinum," etc. Other reports show only aggregated information about donations, such as how much was received per state or country.

A report like this shows the public only a subset of what the charity actually knows about the donations. The full dataset likely includes not only the data reported publicly but also the detailed contact information for each donor, as well as the exact amount that was given, possibly the way the funds were made available, and perhaps notes about the interests of the donor so that interactions can be more personalized. That type of information would not be shared. It can be fairly simple to produce aggregated or lower-resolution reports such as these for small datasets, but difficult for very large ones. That's where a technique like views with chained permissions come in handy.

Situations are commonly encountered in big data settings in which views are useful to manage secure access. Consider, for example, how budget information is handled in a corporation. For a retail business, this data might include inventory SKUs; wholesale costs; warehouse storage information and revenue related to certain product lines; names and social security numbers for employees, as well as their salaries and benefits costs; funds budgeted for marketing and advertising, operations, customer service, and website user experience; and so on. Only a few people in the organization likely would have access to overall budget information, but each department would see totals plus details for their own part of the budget. Some project managers might know aggregated information for personal costs within their department but not be privy to individual salaries or personal information such as Social Security numbers. Usually one department does not see the budget details for other departments. Clearly there are a lot of ways to slice the data within an organization, but very few people are allowed to see everything.

Restricted access is also important for medical data. Many countries have strong privacy rules for the sharing of medical data. Think about who needs to see what information. The billing department likely needs to see details of each patient's name, ID number, account number, procedure ordered and fee, plus the amount that has been paid. Even in that situation, some of the personally identifying information might be masked, such as providing only the last several digits of the Social Security number or credit card numbers for general employees in the accounting department. On the other hand, people in the accounting department would not need to see doctor's notes on medical histories, diagnosis, or outcomes.

The doctor does need access to histories, diagnosis, and outcomes for his or her own patients, along with the patient's name, but would not be allowed to see it for other patients. Furthermore, the doctor might not need or be allowed to see certain types of personally identifying information such as a patient ID number. But a different slice through the medical details is needed for a medical researcher. In that case, the researcher needs to see medical details for many different patients (but none of the billing information). To protect privacy in these situations, the individual patient name and identifying information would not be shared directly. Instead, some masking or a special identifier might be used.

The point is, in each situation, there are a variety of motivations or rules to determine who should be allowed to see what, but regardless of how those needs are defined, it's important to have a reliable tool to let you easily control access. You need to be able to specify the particular subset of data appropriate for each person or group so that you've protected the security of the larger dataset. For big data situations, Apache Drill is particularly attractive among SQL query engines for this purpose. Here's why.

Apache Drill Views for Granular Security

Like the pieces of the treasure map depicted in Figure 3-1, Apache Drill is an excellent tool for managing access to secure data on a need-to-know basis. It is currently the only one of the SQL-on-Hadoop tools that provides views with chained impersonation to control access in a differentially secure manner. Put simply, Drill allows users to delegate access to specific subsets of sensitive data. Before we describe in detail how to create and use Drill views, take a look at some background on this useful tool.

What is Apache Drill? Apache Drill is an open source, open community project that provides a highly scalable SQL query engine with an unusual level of flexibility combined with performance. Drill supports standard ANSI SQL syntax on big data tools including Apache Hadoop-based platforms, Apache HBase (or MapR-DB), and MongoDB. Drill also connects with familiar BI tools such as Tableau, and it can access a wide variety of data formats, including Parquet and JSON, even when nested. Its ability to handle schema-on-the-fly makes Drill a useful choice for data exploration and a way to improve time-to-value through a shorter path for iterative queries, as depicted in Figure 3-3.

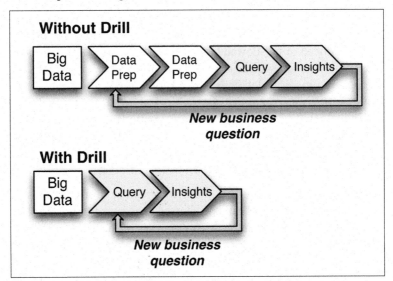

Figure 3-3. Faster time-to-value in big data settings using open source Apache Drill SQL query engine. Using Drill can let you bypass the need for extensive data preparation because of its ability to use a wide

variety of data formats and to recognize a schema without defining it ahead of time. The result is an interactive query process for powerful data exploration.

How Views Work

The basic way views work in Drill is very simple, because all of the security is handled using file system permissions and all of the functionality is handled by Drill itself. The basic idea is that a view is a file that contains a query. Storing the query in a file instead of embedding it as a sub-query gives the view two things: a name, and access permissions that can be controlled by the owner of the view. A Drill view can be used in a query if the user running the query can read the file containing the view. The clever bit is that the view itself can access any data that the owner of the view can access.

Figure 3-4 shows how chained impersonation of views in Drill can be used to control access to data on a very fine-grained level.

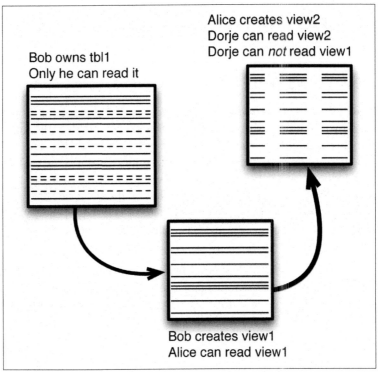

Bob owns tbl1
Only he can read it

Alice creates view2
Dorje can read view2
Dorje can *not* read view1

Bob creates view1
Alice can read view1

Figure 3-4. Drill views allow users to selectively control visibility of data. Bob can allow Alice to see only the solid lines, and she can allow Dorje to see only certain columns of these solid lines. Alice cannot expose the dashed lines.

Here, horizontal lines stand for data. Bob, as the owner of the table, can access any of the data in the table. He can also create a view that only exposes some of the data. Suppose that Bob would like to allow Alice access to the data represented by the solid lines. He can do this by creating a view that Alice can read. Even though Alice cannot read the original data directly, she can use the view Bob created to read the solid-line data.

Moreover, Alice can create a view herself that allows Dorje to have access to an excerpt of the data that Alice can see via Bob's view. Dorje can access neither Bob's view nor the table directly, but by accessing the view that Alice created, he can access some of the data exposed by Bob's view. That happens because Alice's view can access anything Alice can access, which includes Bob's view. Bob's view in turn can access anything that Bob can see. Since Dorje cannot change Bob or Alice's view and Alice can't change Bob's view, the only data that Dorje can see is the subset Alice has permitted, and that is a subset of the data that Bob allowed Alice to see.

Drill views can perform any transformation or filtering that can be done in SQL. This includes filtering rows and selecting columns, of course, but it can also include computing aggregates or calling masking functions. Complex logical constraints can be imposed. For instance, to assist in following German privacy laws, a table that holds IP addresses might mask away the low bits for users with mailing addresses in Germany or if the IP address resolves to a German service provider. One particularly useful thing to do with Drill views is to call commercially available masking (or unmasking) libraries so that privacy policies can be enforced at a very granular level.

Summary of Need-to-Know Methods

This chapter has described some of the motivations and methods for making data available selectively. The key idea is that by using SQL views (in this case, we recommend Apache Drill views), you can easily control what data is visible and what data remains hidden from view. Of course, you must make a careful decision about whether particular subsets of data should be seen as-is, should be masked, or should not be seen—and if you do mask data, you must do it competently. The point is, once you decide what you want to show and what you want to restrict, you can use Apache Drill views with permissions via chained impersonation to carry out your wishes in a reliable way. Users see what you choose for them to see; the remainder of data remains hidden and private.

There are other situations where masking and selective availability as described in this chapter are not acceptable because it is not appropriate to show any of the original data. In those cases, you should consider some of the synthetic data techniques described in later chapters of this book. Synthetic data may allow you to share important, but non-private, aspects of your data without the risks of compromising private data.

CHAPTER 4

Fake Data Gives Real Answers

What do you do when this happens?

Customer: We have sensitive data and a critical query that doesn't run at scale. We need expert assistance. Can you help us?

Experts: We'd be happy to. Can we log into your machine?

Customer: No.

Experts: Can you show us your data?

Customer: No.

Experts: How about a stack trace?

Customer: No.

Customer: Can you help us?

At first glance, it may seem as though the customer in this scenario is being unreasonable, but they're actually being smart and responsible. Their data and the details of their project may indeed be too sensitive to be shared with outside experts like you, and yet they do need help. What's the solution?

A similar problem arises when someone is trying to do secure development of a machine learning system. Machine learning requires an iterative approach that involves training a model, evaluating performance, tuning the model, and trying the process over again. It's often not a straightforward cookbook process, but instead one that requires the data scientist to have a good understanding of the data. The data scientist must be able to interpret the initial results produced by the trained model and use this insight to tweak the knobs of the right algorithm to improve performance and better model reality. In these situations, the project can often benefit from the experience of outside collaborators, but getting this help can be challenging when there is a security perimeter protecting the system, as suggested in Figure 4-1.

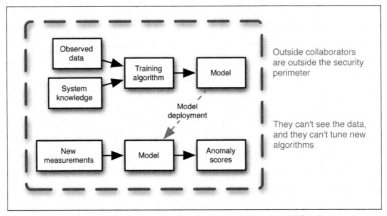

Figure 4-1. The problem: secure development can be difficult. You may want to get help via collaboration with machine learning experts, but how do you do so effectively when they cannot be allowed to see sensitive data stored behind a security perimeter?

Business analysts, data scientists, and data modelers all face this type of problem. The challenge of safely getting outside help is basically the same whether the project involves sophisticated machine learning or much more basic data analytics and engineering. It's a bit like the stories from ancient China in which a learned physician was called in to diagnose an aristocratic female patient. The doctor would enter her chamber and find that the patient was hidden behind an opaque bed curtain. Because the patient was a woman and of high status, the doctor would not have been allowed to see her, and yet he would be expected to make a diagnosis. Reports claim that in this situation the aristocratic lady might have extended one hand and wrist through the opening in the curtain and allowed the physician to take her pulse. He then had to formulate his diagnosis without ever seeing the patient directly or collecting other critical data. To a large extent, he had to guess.

Experts called in to advise a customer on how to fix a broken query or how to tune a model where secure data is involved may feel much like the physician from ancient times. The experts are charged with a task that is seemingly infeasible because of the opaque security curtain barring access to the data in question. They may not even be allowed a "wrist's worth" of a glimpse at the data. But the good news is that they have another approach available to them that the physician did not have: the modern big data expert can make fake data that reveals what they need to know. Here's how this approach works.

The Surprising Thing About Fake Data

Using synthetic data is not in itself a new idea—for instance, it's a fairly standard practice among those who do machine learning to generate synthetic data to test out various algorithms or models before attempting to run them at scale or in production. It's also common to use synthetic data for benchmarking. But synthetic data turns out to be much more valuable than is commonly thought: when used properly, it's a powerful tool for dealing with analytics safely when the data of interest is sensitive and protected behind a security perimeter. What's also surprising in what we're suggesting here is the way we recommend that you generate the data and how you can tell if the synthetic data is a good match for your situation.

The idea in this situation is that instead of providing outsiders with access to sensitive, restricted data, instead you (or they) generate a substitute in the form of custom-built synthetic data. Intuitively, you likely would think that to do this effectively you would need to synthesize fake data that closely matches the characteristics of the real data being analyzed. That's usually very hard to do. Here's where the surprise comes in: exactly matching fake data to the characteristics of the real data usually turns out to be unnecessary.

Matching performance indicators (KPIs) is better than matching data details when generating fake data.

We first saw this pattern while working with a MapR customer, a very large financial company. They were seeking outside help to tune a machine learning model that was using a k-nearest neighbor algorithm. This type of machine learning model can be used for classification, in which you emulate human decisions to assign new data into pre-defined categories, or for fraud detection (perhaps using clustering). In the case of this financial customer, the data being analyzed could not be shown to an outside collaborator, so we generated synthetic data to use as a stand-in. And that led to a surprising observation: even though the synthetic data was not at all a realistic match for the characteristics of the original data, we were able to adjust the synthetic data so that the key performance indices (KPIs) for the model were similar whether we used real or fake data, and that turned out to be all that was needed. Fake data that matched real data with regard to KPIs was good enough to be used for training and tuning the machine learning model, as illustrated in Figure 4-2.

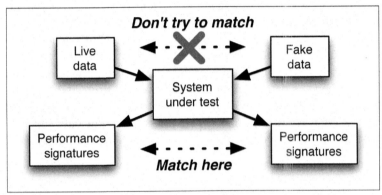

Figure 4-2. When is the fake data you've generated good enough? When it behaves like real data according to the system under test. It's not the match between specific characteristics of the real and fake data that you need to aim for. Instead, it's the comparison of KPIs that matters.

This approach of generating fake data with performance indicators similar to what the customer saw with real data made it possible for them to work with outside collaborators (that is, us) through iterative cycles of evaluation and tuning that are typical of effective machine learning. Once it was established inside the security perimeter that a particular version of synthetic data matched KPIs sufficiently well in the context of the current model training algorithms, the fake data was then used outside the security barrier to build new and improved versions of the model of interest. Those models in turn were subsequently trained and tested on the real data, within the security perimeter, in order to verify that the KPIs still matched well, as outlined in Figure 4-3. This approach allowed development of algorithms and software to proceed without outsiders having access to sensitive data but still with a very high degree of confidence that the algorithm would work the same on real data as it had on synthetic data.

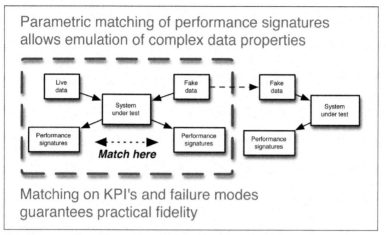

Figure 4-3. When the KPIs match well enough for fake versus real data, the fake data can then be used for experimenting with the process of interest—in this case, tuning a machine-learning model.

Keep It Simple: log-synth

The program used to generate simulated data in the preceding financial use case was fairly specialized, but this approach of using fake data as a way to work outside a security perimeter showed great promise. In order to make this method practical in a larger sense, what was needed was a convenient way to generate synthetic data for a variety of situations. For this purpose, Ted Dunning, co-author of this book, wrote a new program called log-synth and made it available as open source software. It is not a large project, so it's just provided via Github (*https://github.com/tdunning/logsynth*).

 Log-synth provides a safe way to get the benefits of data sharing: you never actually give out the real data.

As in the earlier example, the goal of using log-synth is to prepare a dataset that is sufficient to stand in for secure data you do not want to share directly with outsiders. Instead, you just provide specifications for synthesizing appropriate fake data. And as with the earlier data generator, to use log-synth effectively, you should look for a match with key performance indicators exhibited by original data and the process in question rather than a match with exact characteristics of the real data, as previously shown in Figure 4-2.

Log-synth is simple yet powerful, and it can be easily adjusted to suit your own needs. The program comes pre-packaged with the ability to simulate realistic data for a wide range of kinds of data. There are a number of different samplers that let you customize the fake data that you generate. Figure 4-4 shows some of the options.

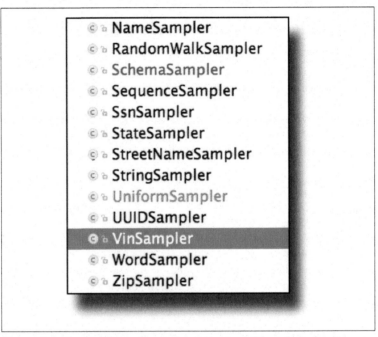

Figure 4-4. Log-synth can be easily customized. The selected option here provides generation of realistic vehicle identification data (VIN). Other options include generation of realistic names of people, US-style social security numbers (SSN), street names, and so on. For the VIN, Zip, and SSN samplers, considerable amounts of additional data is available with each sample beyond the basic number.

Figure 4-5 displays an excerpt of log-synth schema as an example of how simply it can be configured. For specialized situations, log-synth also is extensible, as we show in Chapter 6.

```
{
  // generates lists with exactly 5 samples each
  "name": "fixed-length",
  "class":"sequence",
  "lengthDistribution":5
  "base": ...
}
```

Figure 4-5. The open source log-synth program can be easily adjusted to fit the particular situation of interest. Shown here is partial schema that would be used to generate fake data with values that are sequences of a particular fixed length.

Generating synthetic data can be useful even in certain types of in-house analyses. For instance, during testing, it is useful to have sample databases of different sizes, but to down-sample large relational datasets without losing meaningful connections can be difficult. Instead, synthesizing sample datasets from scratch with all necessary linkages can actually be much easier. But the main advantage of log-synth is for dealing with the safe management of data security when outsiders need to interact with sensitive data in complex ways. Log-synth makes this interaction possible even when you can't share the real thing.

This approach is not just theoretical. It's already proven useful in real-world use cases involving secure data. Before going on to learn exactly how to use log-synth in Chapters 5–7, look at the following two different ways that it has been used in the real world. The first use case is a basic approach, and the second use case employs log-synth with extensions.

Log-synth Use Case 1: Broken Large-Scale Hive Query

This first log-synth use case is a real-life version of the scenario described at the opening of this chapter. The MapR customer was a large insurance company. Naturally, they held sensitive data that could not be shared directly with outsiders. The situation involved a very long and complicated Hive query the customer needed to run against a large-scale dataset—the problem was, the query was broken.

Initially, the customer had tried to down-sample the data in order to make it easier to work on fixing the query, but in this case, down-sampling wasn't a feasible course of action because of the number of tables and relationships in the data. They were working with complex relational data, and down-sampling messed up the relationships. At this point, the customer wanted to get outside help for dealing with the broken query, and they turned to MapR for advice. This is where log-synth came into play.

The customer explained that because of data security, they could not permit logging in to their system by outsiders, nor could they provide access to real data or even stack traces that might have given clues to how and why the Hive query wasn't running properly. Instead, we worked with them to create synthetic data that exhibited the same problematic behavior from Hive. In order to use log-synth effectively in this situation, the customer started off by providing a rough description of data size and gave us a copy of the database schema, but no sample of real data was provided.

The collaboration fell into these two stages:

- **Stage 1: Prepare to collaborate:** Generate appropriate fake data that could realistically emulate the behavior of the real data so that outsiders have a way to collaborate.
- **Stage 2: Fix the broken query:** Work outside the security perimeter using fake data in order to find the bug in the query and fix it.

The steps in preparing to collaborate (Stage 1) are shown in Figure 4-6. The process started in Step 1 with an attempt to run the Hive query on real data in order to see the failure profile (in this case, the failure mode is the KPI). Next, in Step 2, the customer transferred the schema for this table outside the security perimeter to be available to us, the outside collaborators from MapR. In Step 3, we used this real schema information to design the log-synth-specific schema that was needed in order to synthesize an appropriate fake dataset. Step 4 used log-synth to generate a fake dataset.

Now we had synthetic material on which to work, but would this fake data provide an appropriate input for working on the query? Before starting that phase of the work, the usefulness of the fake data had to be verified. To do this, the customer provided us with the broken Hive query, as shown in Step 5 of the diagram in Figure 4-6. When the original Hive query was run against the newly generated fake data (Step 6), the result was the same failure signature as with the real data. In other words, we had found a match between the KPIs for the fake data and the real data. Put informally, if it breaks the same, it's as good as the same.

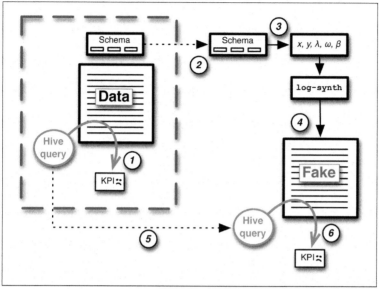

Figure 4-6. A step-wise look at Stage 1 of collaboration to fix a complex Hive query for secured data. The goal was to set up a way for collaborators to work outside the security perimeter. To make this possible, the customer provided a portion of their schema to inform the process of generating fake data using log-synth. Because the original Hive query broke the same way on the fake data as it did with real data, the fake data could be used instead of the real data.

Keep in mind that the fake data didn't match the real data in any way except that it had the same data types, sizes, and—most importantly —the same failure modes.

Stage 2 of the collaboration process involved having us (the outside collaborators) do the job the customer had brought us in to do. We were able to look at stack traces we had generated to track down the problem, which turned out to be a bug in Hive. We modified Hive and tested against the fake dataset to see that the query ran to completion on the fake data. The process up to this point is depicted as Step 1 of the diagram presented in Figure 4-7. Once the problem with Hive was fixed, the patched version of Hive was pulled back inside the security perimeter and tested on the real data (Steps 2 and 3). That test succeeded, so we knew we had a real fix.

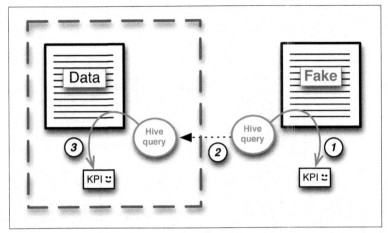

Figure 4-7. Stage 2 of the collaboration between an insurance company and outside collaborators (MapR) to fix a bug in Hive found using a large-scale secure dataset. Because appropriate fake data was generated in Stage 1 of the process (Figure 4-6), in Stage 2 the outside experts could work outside the security perimeter to repair the bug in Hive so that the query could run properly on the secured real data back inside the perimeter.

The final result was that despite the need for the insurance company to keep their data unobserved behind the security perimeter, they were able to safely take advantage of outside expertise in order to find and fix the problem. Thanks to log-synth, they essentially shared access to the essence of what mattered in the data without outsiders ever having to actually see the real data.

This real-world use case demonstrates the usefulness of the open source log-synth program for safely carrying out large-scale data analytics in a secure environment. The same approach can be used in a wide variety of situations, especially because log-synth can be conveniently adjusted to produce customized fake data with the desired behavior to be realistic relative to the secure system of interest. Chapter 5 provides a detailed technical description of how this particular use case was implemented, and Chapter 7 gives tips for putting log-synth to work in your own situation.

In addition to these basic ways to use log-synth, you also can extend it for use in secure environments on more complex problems. That was what happened in our next fake data use case.

Log-synth Use Case 2: Fraud Detection Model for Common Point of Compromise

Log-synth is written in Java, and it's relatively easy for someone who is comfortable with Java to extend log-synth to work well in a wider scope of use cases. One real-world example of that type of extension was the use of log-synth to help a large financial institution improve their fraud detection—in particular, to identify a merchant that was a common point of compromise. Before we look at what happened with this use case, here's some background on the type of fraud in question.

What Thieves Do

Thieves have developed a clever method for the particular type of fraud that is the focus of this use case. They steal financial account numbers such as credit or debit card numbers by breaching a merchant's data security. They might do this by skimming credit card numbers using false readers, by a point of sale virus installed on cash registers, or through a variety of other techniques. The issue is, at some point in time, the bad guys get access to financial account information for many consumers and then they go to work making fraudulent purchases.

That's where the thieves do something really clever. In the old style of financial card fraud, the thief would steal a card number and then quickly make really big purchases before the account breach was reported and the card was shut down. In the new style of card fraud, thieves steal account information, often from many consumers at one time, and then *make a huge number of small fraudulent purchases*. Even if each fraudulent transaction is for only a small amount, perhaps $10–$25 equivalent for US currency, the total amount stolen adds up to millions of dollars when it's happening to thousands or even millions of accounts. The clever thing is that because each transaction is relatively small, consumers are much less likely to notice them or report them, so it's much harder to track down the point of compromise.

Why Machine Learning Experts Were Consulted

In this log-synth use case, the MapR customer asked for help improving their fraud detection model because they wanted to be able to identify more fraudulent transactions and to react faster than previously. This would help them identify the source of the breach as well as to close down compromised accounts faster, therefore limiting losses. As with the previous example, the customer had sensitive data and could not provide access to the MapR experts (us again) they wanted to consult. Log-synth to the rescue.

The financial customer had large-scale behavioral data on merchant transactions for individual consumers. For this problem, we transformed the data the customer had into a timeline of purchases for each consumer. Each timeline showed every merchant with whom a particular consumer conducted a business transaction, as well as the time of the transaction. The latter information is important to be able to identify which merchants were visited before a reported fraudulent purchase. The model was built to look for one or more merchants who appeared in a transaction more often than expected anywhere upstream from known fraud.

There are several reasons why this case is a hard problem to solve. One reason is that many frauds are small and therefore often go unreported. Another difficulty is that there are other sources of fraud unrelated to the compromise that cause a steady background of fraud reports. In other words, there is a lot of background noise that must be dealt with.

Using log-synth to Generate Fake User Histories

Back to the real-world use case. We wrote extensions to log-synth to enable it to generate fake user histories with made-up merchants so we could conduct common point of compromise simulations. The details of how this was done are discussed in Chapter 6. The results of the simulation were dramatic, as shown in Figure 4-8. Working with the fake data, the model identified a merchant with an exceptionally high breach score, which you can see marked in the figure. As it turned out, this merchant was exactly the one that was "compromised" in the simulations.

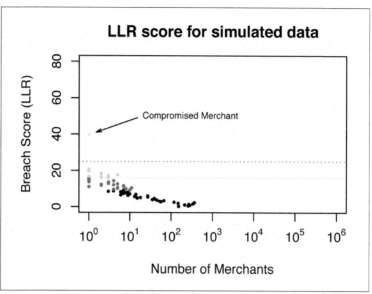

Figure 4-8. Fake data was generated using the log-synth program to match the performance signatures of the real data to find potential fraud in a merchant compromise scenario. Merchants were grouped by score. The group average score was graphed against the number of merchants in each group, and an extreme outlier popped out of the simulated data.

The use of fake data generated by log-synth let us build and tune a model appropriate for the customer's goals without the customer ever having to show us any of the real data. Having demonstrated the potential for this model, it was then used by the customer on data inside their security perimeter. The real results were even more dramatic: the model identified a real merchant with an exceptionally high breach score, one over 80, as you can see in the graphical results in Figure 4-9.

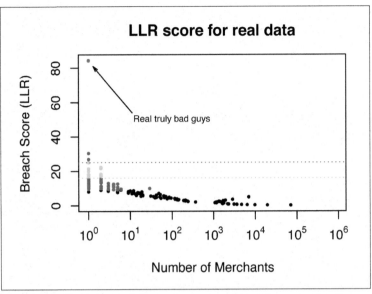

Figure 4-9. Once the model was shown to work with appropriately synthesized fake data, the analysis was conducted on real data inside the security perimeter. The results for this real-world use case are even more dramatic than with the simulated data: notice the single merchant that showed up with a breach score over 80. This merchant turned out to be a serious point of compromise.

This story is not a hypothetical exercise; it's a real-world use case. Seeing the high breach score for the merchant in question, the financial institution notified the US Secret Service, and an investigation took place. The merchant, a restaurant, was in fact seriously compromised and was the source of considerable amounts of fraud. In an odd twist of fate, the restaurant happened to be close to the residence of an executive of the financial company conducting the fraud detection. Needless to say, the results of this project caught his attention!

Summary: Fake Data and log-synth to Safely Work with Secure Data

The methods described in this chapter give you a simple but powerful way to safely work with outsiders even when you have highly sensitive data that is kept under a security barrier. You can get the benefit of their help in a way that is specific to your project *without ever having to show them your data*. The key is to generate fake data that produces realistic results with the process or system in question.

The most surprising thing about this approach is that *the fake data doesn't need to match the characteristics of real data exactly*. That data-to-data feature matching is very hard to build into synthetic data, so it's good news that it's generally not needed. Instead, you just have to *match KPIs between fake and real data when used as input for the process of interest*. Note that these KPIs are relative to the specific problem and models you are working with.

It's also good news that you don't need a highly sophisticated, fancy version of data generation to do this. We provide links to code for a *simple but powerful open source data synthesizer called log-synth* that was developed by the author. This program is available to you via Github.

You can easily adjust the data you generate to fit your particular situation using *convenient samplers that are pre-packaged with the base version of log-synth*. In addition, log-synth can be used in an even wider range of settings by writing Java-based extensions to the original code. One such extension, a *common point of compromise simulator, is already available with log-synth on Github*.

One of the safest ways to share sensitive data publicly or with outside consultants is to provide a way for them to deal with the data without ever actually seeing it. That's what the use of custom-generated fake data and log-synth let you do.

Detailed explanations of the two real-world use cases based on log-synth that were mentioned here are provided in Chapters 5–7, as are implementation details for using log-synth in general.

CHAPTER 5

Fixing a Broken Large-Scale Query

The use of customized synthetic data as a way to safely work with outsiders when dealing with sensitive, secure data was discussed in Chapter 4, and we mentioned an open source tool, log-synth, as a simple but powerful data generator. In order to demonstrate the effectiveness of this approach, we also introduced two real-world use cases that benefited from log-synth. In the current chapter, we go into much more detail about the implementation of one of those use cases, fixing the problem encountered when an insurance company tried to run a complex Hive query being used with secure data.

In addition to more fully explaining the insurance company use case, we go into details in this chapter to show you how you can use this type of example more generically, beyond this particular sector. You should be able to apply the same approach to related situations in your own projects. It's not just about one bug in Hive—it's more importantly about how to use log-synth–generated, simulated data to work in a secure environment with complex queries against large-scale relational data.

A Description of the Problem

In the case of the insurance company, the customer had a query that involved a join of more than 20 tables and included a sub-query as well. This query was simplified from a larger query that had also caused problems. In order to reproduce the problem, we needed to have test data that emulated the structure and scale of the original in order to observe the bug. As it turned out, the actual bug only showed up when the query optimizer made certain decisions, and those decisions were driven by the sizes of the tables in question in relation to each other.

The customer was unwilling to share even masked data, both due to the size and the possibility of inadvertent disclosure of private data. Stack traces were also considered impossible to release due to the fact that it was not clear what private data might be inadvertently included. Determining whether or not the stack traces included anything private would have required an infeasible amount of additional analysis—even if the stack traces had no sensitive data, releasing them would require a security review, which would take too long. Synthetic data was the only option.

Determining What the Synthetic Data Needed to Be

The original data for this use case was large-scale relational data. Once it was determined that synthetic data was needed in order to take advantage of the collaboration of experts outside the security perimeter (us), the next step was to decide exactly what the synthetic data needed to look like. Unfortunately, it wasn't just a matter of creating random fake data and sticking it into a comma-separated format. The bug being chased only appeared when the query optimizer saw a particular pattern of query and input data statistics. Also, in order for the query to do anything at all, the data had to join correctly across all of the foreign key relations in the data. These factors meant that the data had to replicate some aspects of the original data without actually being some kind of replica or resampling of the original data.

We decided to not replicate every detail of the data, but to focus on the general shape of the data in terms of number of rows and columns, the linkage between tables, and the frequency skew in the join keys between tables.

Guaranteeing referential integrity for the join keys was important. Fortunately, with synthetic data, it was actually fairly simple to guarantee this since all of the join keys were integers, as is quite commonly the case. We simply generated consecutive integers as keys in the dimension tables. That meant that all of the integers from zero up to the number of rows in the dimension table were valid keys, and we could therefore generate a valid reference by picking any integer in that range.

For the largest tables, we needed to generate several billion rows of data. This process can be parallelized trivially by breaking the overall generation into ranges that are generated independently. A single machine can generate relatively simple table structures at tens of thousands of rows per second per core. Even a single machine can thus generate a billion rows by using a number of threads. With a moderate-sized cluster, even trillion-row tables are not hard to generate.

In the end, it was clear that the only critical characteristic of the actual customer data that we had to replicate was that it stimulated the bug in the query optimizer. All other aspects were irrelevant. In other words, the key performance indicator was the occurrence of the bug. All other characteristics of the data other than the KPI were irrelevant. The only thing that mattered about the synthetic data was that the KPI matched, as depicted back in Figure 4-2.

Furthermore, once we developed a generator for data that caused the fault to occur, we could adjust the specification of the data, making small changes while preserving the fault-inducing nature of the data. This process ultimately resulted in the development of a tiny dataset that would induce the fault, and that in turn allowed engineers to quickly find and fix the core problem in the query optimizer. Down-sampling real data is often quite difficult because of transitive relations between records, but making the synthetic data smaller was relatively easy because all that was required was to generate less data. Because referential integrity of the data was guaranteed, the only remaining question was whether the key indicator of stimulating the bug was preserved.

Schema for the Synthetic Data

Because the original schema was large and unwieldy, not to mention proprietary, we will illustrate the data synthesis process here using a schema that has a similar but much simpler structure.

The simpler schema we use in this chapter is an instance of a star schema, as you can see in Figure 5-1. A star schema has a central table known as the fact table, which contains a little bit of actual data (the measures) and mostly contains references to other tables (the dimensions). The example here will use a very much-simplified star schema that involves sales of individual products. The fact table records each sale and references customer, item, time, and store tables. The fact table also records the exact time of the sale, the quantity, unit price, and any discount. Figure 5-1 illustrates the structure of these tables.

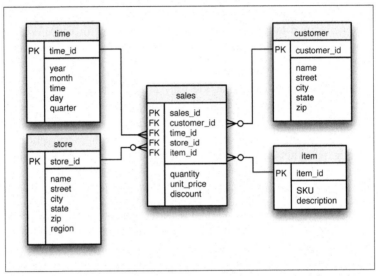

Figure 5-1. In this star schema, the sales table is the fact table, and it is linked to dimension tables. For each row of each dimension table, there can be more than one row in the sales table. For the store, customer, and item dimensions, there may not be any sales, so the linkage is zero-or-more.

The original problem was that a large join query inside a sub-query failed to run because the query planner crashed before the query was actually executed. Moreover, since the problem was a planner failure, the statistics of the tables had to be somewhat realistic, at least as far as the optimizer could tell. In the sample schema in Figure 5-1, for instance, this would mean that the sales table would have substantially more rows than any other table, that the number of customers would be larger than the number of stores, and that there are more items than either customers or stores. For Hive and most other Hadoop-based query tools, matching statistics usually only means that the tables are the right size, but it could require that skew in the distribution of join keys matches reasonably as well.

The open source log-synth project was designed with this sort of synthetic data generation in mind. As a result, data for the schemas like the one shown in Figure 5-1 can be generated fairly easily using log-synth.

Log-synth requires a specification of the data to be generated for each table. In building these specifications, we can start with any table in the schema. Probably the simplest is the customer table. Example 5-1 shows one possible way to generate customer data. This log-synth schema is in the form of a JSON list that specifies the fields to be generated and what kind of data to generate.

Example 5-1. One possible log-synth schema for the customer table (one of the dimension tables) from the star-schema from Figure 5-1.

```
[
    {"name":"customer_id", "class":"id"},
    {"name":"name", "class":"name", "type":"first_last"},
    {"name":"street", "class":"address"},
    {"class":"flatten", "value": {
        "class":"zip", "fields":"city,state,zip"}}
]
```

In this schema, we have three fields: customer_id, name, and street, that are generated directly as, respectively, a sequence of consecutive integers, names, and street addresses. These fields are trivial to generate because they can be generated completely independently. The fourth clause in the schema is a bit fancier. Notice the use of flatten there. What is happening here is that the data generated by log-synth consists of a sequence of JSON objects that can contain complex, nested data. When the consumer of the random data wants pure relational data, nested data isn't what we want. On the other hand, the log-synth zip sampler returns a complex object that can contain, among other fields, city, state, and ZIP code.

The reason behind that is that we would like to have a city, state, and ZIP code that make sense together. In log-synth, the easy way to do this is to generate a ZIP code with associated city and state. This will give us the fields we want with the appropriate correlations, but it will leave the fields we want buried in a JSON object inside a field in the generated record. The solution is to flatten the result of the ZIP code object so that the individual city, state, and ZIP code fields are at the top level in the resulting data.

Generating the Synthetic Data

This schema can be used to generate data with a log-synth command like the following:

```
log-synth -schema customer.synth -count 50k -format csv
```

Example 5-2 displays some sample data that was generated by the schema in Example 5-1.

Example 5-2. Flattening synthetic data: this sample was generated by log-synth using the schema shown in Example 5-1.

```
customer_id,name,street,zip,city,state
0,"Mark Long","8578 Pied River Flats","02630","BARNSTABLE","MA"
1,"Chris Lanier","90018 Lost Treasure Corner","06083","ENFIELD","CT"
2,"Bryant Brandon","30712 Bright Shadow Stroll","93922","CARMEL","CA"
3,"Norman Horn","66871 Dewy Bird Shoal","59727","DIVIDE","MT"
4,"Carmen Nowell","6053 Velvet Barn Glen","29329","CONVERSE","SC"
```

The rows for the synthetic data in Example 5-2 are in CSV format. They could just as easily have been generated in tab-delimited form or JSON. Support for XML with log-synth is currently under development.

Without flattening the data, the results would be more like what is depicted in Example 5-3. Notice the way that the street, city, state, and ZIP are at different nesting levels. This shows why the flattening process is a good idea.

Example 5-3. Without flattening, data generated using the zip sampler is nested, but street address is not. For use with relational, it helps to flatten this structure.

```
{"customer_id":0,"name":"Terrence Wheeler",
 "street":"15547 Golden Anchor Glen",
 "address":{"zip":"85240","city":"QUEEN CREEK","state":"AZ"}}
{"customer_id":1,"name":"Duane Morgan",
 "street":"11353 Sleepy Shadow Pike",
 "address":{"zip":"59825","city":"CLINTON","state":"MT"}}
{"customer_id":2,"name":"Heath Davison",
 "street":"93544 Quiet Pumpkin Canyon",
 "address":{"zip":"47352","city":"LEWISVILLE","state":"IN"}}
{"customer_id":3,"name":"Jeffrey Dellinger",
 "street":"39119 Colonial Crow Dale",
 "address":{"zip":"57584","city":"WITTEN","state":"SD"}}
{"customer_id":4,"name":"Mitzi Michael",
```

```
"street":"24468 Windy Wagon Crest",
"address":{"zip":"60129","city":"ESMOND","state":"IL"}}
```

Let's apply the same ideas to another part of the star schema, the store table. Example 5-4 shows how the store table can be generated very similarly.

Example 5-4. Schema used for generating the store table.

```
[
    {"name":"store_id", "class":"id"},
    {"name":"street", "class":"address"},
    {"class":"flatten", "value": {
        "class":"zip", "fields":"city,state,zip"}}
]
```

The time table uses a similar flattening trick to generate records with multiple fields regarding times that move forward at semi-random intervals (see Example 5-5). Here, the event sampler generates event times at a rate of about once per 10 days, and the year, month, and day of the resulting times are output as separate fields that are then flattened.

Example 5-5. Schema for generating synthetic data for the time table.

```
[
    {"name":"time_id", "class":"id"},
    {"class":"flatten", "value": {
        "class": "event",
        "rate": "0.1/d",
        "fields": {
            "year": "yyyy",
            "month": "MM",
            "day": "dd"
        }}
    }
]
```

In the star schema for this use case, the fact table is the sales table (Figure 5-1). The sales table is slightly more elaborate because it has to have references to the other tables. This additional feature is handled by using a sampler that picks integers from a limited range. Given that we know how many records we generated for the dimension tables, this is pretty straightforward. The schema for the fact table is shown in Example 5-6.

Example 5-6. Schema for the fact table in the star schema; in this case, it is the sales table.

```
[
    {"name":"sales_id", "class":"id"},
    {"name":"customer_id", "class":"foreign-key", "size":1000},
    {"name":"time_id", "class":"foreign-key", "size":10000},
    {"name":"store_id", "class":"foreign-key", "size":100},
    {"name":"item_id", "class":"foreign-key", "size":100000},

    {"name":"quantity", "class":"int", "skew":0.5},
    {"name":"unit_price", "class":"gamma", "dof":1, "scale":10},
    {"name":"discount", "class":"uniform", "min":0, "max":20},
    {"name":"exact_time", "class":"event",
        "start": "2014-01-01", "format":"yyyy-MM-dd HH:mm:ss",
        "rate": "10/d"}
]
```

Tips and Caveats

There are a few things to note here. First, the values of exact_time in the sales records will have no correlation to the times we put into the time table. This means that some of the queries that we might try would produce moderate levels of gibberish. Had we really cared (and for this particular use case, we don't), the typical approach would be to generate data for the sales table in JSON form, including the fields that we want to peel off into the time dimension table. We could then extract the necessary data into the final sales and time tables using a tool such as Apache Drill that can handle JSON as input and produce tables. In general, fact and dimension tables are not supposed to contain redundant information, but in a few cases such as this one, we do have correlations that we can choose whether or not to preserve. Whether we do preserve correlations like this depends on whether the correlations impact the KPIs we have chosen. If not, there is no need to complicate the synthesis of the data.

Another issue is that we have hard-coded the sizes of the various dimension tables. In practice, this is normally handled by simply writing a script in Python or bash that inserts sizes into templates for the schema tables and into the log-synth commands. This allows flexibility without complicating the design of log-synth itself. An example of such a script can be found in the sample code for this book in *src/main/log-synth/generate.py*.

When using this kind of table generation to replicate a failure, what typically happens is that the fault of interest will be encountered when a full-scale dataset is processed, but the same fault can also be induced for much smaller datasets as well, if certain size or skew relationships are maintained. This is what happened in real life. The original fault only showed up with inputs on the scale of billions of rows, but once we had a tool to generate synthetic data, the size could carefully be trimmed down. Ultimately, a test set with only a half-dozen tables and about a thousand rows was identified, which caused the same fault. Having a small test example made it easy to find the error and fix it. Put in general terms, down-sampling for relational data is hard; generating less data is easy.

What to Do from Here?

In the use case that we described here, we were able to generate data quickly and easily. That would very likely have been impossible if we had tried to include all of the possible cross-correlations and other subtle features of the original data. In contrast, we matched a very simple performance indicator: whether our test query caused Hive to crash. By focusing our efforts on such a simple performance indicator, we avoided having to model most of the complexities of the original data.

The result was that the generation of the synthetic data we used was nearly trivial. In fact, the simplicity of generating the data is a consequence of our focus only on what was important to us for the problem at hand.

The lesson that can be taken from our experience is that focus is good for simplicity. By limiting the scope of the KPIs that we are trying to replicate, we create degrees of freedom that allow us to simplify the data-generation process. Not all cases will allow the generation to be as easy as it was in this example, but many will be. It is definitely worth starting simple. And it is definitely worth adding synthetic data generation to your bag of tricks.

CHAPTER 6

Fraud Detection

Generating relational data as in the previous chapter is very useful, but there are also many cases where the samplers packaged into the base log-synth system are simply not sufficient for simulating certain kinds of data.

This is particularly true when we need to generate stateful transactional histories, largely because maintaining and modifying the state is really much easier with the capabilities of a full programming language to draw on. Common use cases where this approach is needed include network monitoring (different sources will produce different kinds of events), marine or air position tracking (different craft often have to have tracks that reflect realistic physics), and financial transaction generation (different consumers behave differently and may change their behavior). The key aspect of all stateful transaction streams is that the next transaction depends on current state and the current state changes as a result of transactions. We specifically chose to not have a real programming language of log-synth schema definitions, so you need something more powerful.

Simply defining a new sampler in Java and then referencing that sampler in a schema can handle these stateful use cases fairly easily, however. Log-synth already includes one such sampler, the `common-point-of-compromise`, and you can use it as a template to design other extensions. But first, we describe how this sampler works and how it was used in the real-world fraud example that we described in Chapter 4.

With the common point of compromise use case, we want to use log-synth to generate transaction histories. These transaction histories can be fed into a model that is intended to detect the breach at the merchant who was the original point of compromise for consumer data. Figure 6-1 illustrates this data flow.

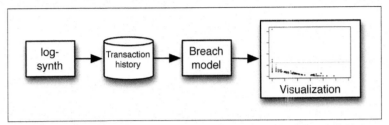

Figure 6-1. We use log-synth to generate a transaction history for a number of consumers. This transaction history will be processed by a breach model whose aim is to find the original point of compromise of customer data.

The goal here, of course, is to be able to help modelers develop new breach models without letting them see any real data, because that data is too sensitive to expose to outsiders. A description of the type of fraudulent behavior to be targeted by the detection model was given in Chapter 4.

What Is Really Important?

Keep in mind that the yardstick to judge whether or not the data you generate is good enough for a particular situation is the degree of matching between the KPIs for a particular process when comparing fake data and real data as input. This idea was explained in Chapter 4 and illustrated in Figure 4-1. But how do you know which KPIs matter?

As we model the transaction histories, the performance signatures that we will need to match include the distribution of the breach model scores and the degree to which the compromised merchant can be identified. We will also need to roughly match simpler performance signatures such as the number of consumers and merchants and the distributions of the number of transactions consumers make and merchants receive.

The breach model attempts to find the compromised merchant by looking for which merchants are over-represented in the histories of consumers whose histories have a fraud in them. Merchants who appear significantly more often among the transactions prior to a detected fraud should be considered to be possibly compromised. The job of the breach model is made harder because frauds occur sporadically even in uncompromised accounts, and because not all compromised accounts will have a detected fraud.

Note that the inner workings of the fraudsters and the fraud detection model aren't visible in the performance signature. The failure modes of the fraud model are also invisible. All that matters here is that fraud is detected more after a compromise, and that it is detected at a non-zero rate even without a compromise. What this means is that our transaction sampler doesn't need to have any details on the transaction and doesn't need to model any of the actual mechanisms by which fraud occurs. Nor does it have to model any of the mechanisms of the fraud detection model itself.

In a similar way, the traffic patterns and seasonality of transactions are also not part of the performance signature. The simulated consumers here transact day and night at a statistically consistent rate. Real transactions rates vary by day, by week, or by season, but none of that is visible in the performance signature, so none of those effects have to be respected by the transaction sampler. What we are doing is narrowing down what needs to match in the KPIs. This will massively simplify the process of matching the synthetic data performance signature to the performance signature from real data.

Key Idea

It's essential to include in the performance signature only those performance indices that measure what is really important. This limitation allows more degrees of freedom in the random data generator, which in turn makes it much easier to find suitable parameters for the generator. This approach also makes the generator vastly simpler.

This pattern of only paying attention to details that affect the performance signature is a critical characteristic of how we recommend that you generate simulated data. If it isn't visible in the performance signature, you don't have to model it. If some characteristic of the data really is important, then you need to make sure that something in the performance signature reflects that characteristic.

The User Model

The state model used in the common point of compromise sampler is illustrated in Figure 6-2. The idea here is that consumers each have their own independent timeline, represented by an arrow. These consumers have transactions with various merchants represented by rectangles. After consumer data is compromised by transacting with merchant *m0*, the consumers have an elevated risk of fraud, but it is possible that no fraud will be observed even after a consumer's data has been compromised. Also, there is a background level of unrelated fraud to take into account. For this reason, some consumers who never visited the compromised merchant may still be subject to a fraudulent event.

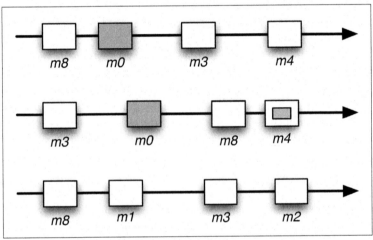

Figure 6-2. The meaning of data used in the common point of compromise example. Each user is illustrated here as a separate timeline that proceeds from left to right. Users transact with different merchants m0...m8 at different times. Users who transact with merchant m0, marked in grey, thereafter have an elevated risk of fraud. A subsequent fraud event (with the middle consumer at merchant m4) is marked here as a rectangle with a grey core.

Sampler for the Common Point of Compromise

The following code is a slightly simplified version of the actual code in the `CommonPointOfCompromise` class in log-synth, and it shows how the state of a consumer, consisting of a single flag that indicates whether the consumer's data has been compromised, evolves over time:

```
boolean compromised = true;
List<Transaction> history = new ArrayList<>();
while (t < end) {
    int merchantId = merchant.sample();
    if (isCompromisePeriod() && merchant_id == 0) {
        compromised = true;
    }
    double pFraud;
    if (isExploitPeriod() && compromised) {
        pFraud = COMPROMISED_FRAUD_RATE;
    } else {
        pFraud = UNCOMPROMISED_FRAUD_RATE;
    }
    fraudDetected = (rand.nextDouble() < pFraud) ? 1 : 0;
    history.add(new Transaction(t, merchantId, fraudDetected));

    t += timeStep.sample();
}
```

This code is extremely simple—far simpler than it would be if we needed to have a complete model of how different kinds of fraud occurs and how it is detected. In this simulation, in contrast, all we need to know is what the detection rates for compromised and uncompromised accounts are. We also don't need to include any information about users or about merchants other than merchant identifiers and the fact that some merchants are more popular than others. The distribution of transactions to merchants is handled by delegating to the `merchant` sampler, whose implementation is provided by the log-synth framework.

This sort of state transition is very easy to express in Java but impossible to generate using just the other samplers in log-synth and would be very difficult to express cleanly in SQL. Happily, it is very easy to integrate a new sampler into log-synth, so we can switch between methods very easily.

It is important to notice that each time this sampler is called, the returned value is an entire history for a single user. This history could easily contain thousands of transactions or more. As a result, records are produced more slowly than in cases with much simpler records, as was the case for the simulations described in Chapter 5. That said, even a fairly moderate machine can generate a million or so transactions per second (equivalent to 5,000 users per second and almost 100MB/s of data). A large cluster of machines could easily generate hundreds of millions of simulated transactions per second.

For the purposes of this simulation, we define a time period during which compromises can happen, and also a period of time during which fraud due to the compromise can happen. These time periods are independent and could conceivably overlap. These two time periods are depicted in Figure 6-3.

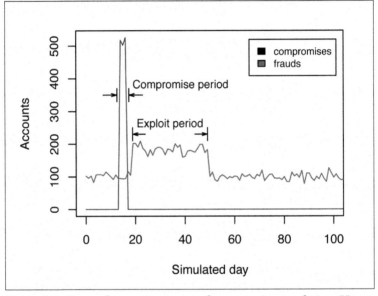

Figure 6-3. Trace of a common point of compromise simulation. Here the number of accounts compromised is shown as the black line. This number spikes during the compromise period, but is zero elsewhere. During the exploit period, the amount of detected fraud increases above the background level due to fraud being committed against compromised accounts.

The figure shows a trace of such a simulation that involves 50,000 simulated users. During days 17 through 19, consumers who transact with merchant 0 are compromised. During days 20–49, transactions by consumers who are compromised have a higher chance of being marked as fraud. From day 50 onwards, being compromised has no effect. During the entire time, sporadic fraud unrelated to compromised data is detected at a background level of about 100 accounts per day.

How the Breach Model Works

The goal of this use case is to develop a breach model that can detect merchants with a high likelihood of being compromised, based on the pattern of victimized user transactions. The breach model used here is actually fairly simple. What it does is to compute a score for each merchant based on four counts specific to that merchant. These counts include:

- The number of consumers where the merchant was seen preceding a fraud (k_{11})
- The number of consumers where the merchant was seen with no fraud afterwards (k_{12})
- The number of consumers where the merchant was not seen and where fraud was detected (k_{21})
- The number of consumers where the merchant was not seen and where no fraud was detected (k_{22})

These numbers are typically arranged in a table where columns represent whether fraud was noted and rows represent whether or not the merchant had a transaction with a consumer (see Figure 6-4). The counts in the table count the number of users for each combination of conditions. That is, the upper left of the table contains k_{11}, the number of consumers where fraud was reported and where the consumers transacted with the merchant of interest before the fraudulent transaction.

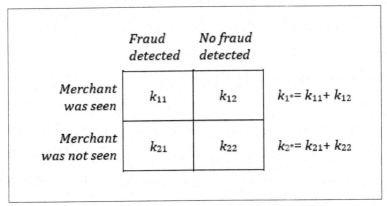

	Fraud detected	No fraud detected	
Merchant was seen	k_{11}	k_{12}	$k_{1*} = k_{11} + k_{12}$
Merchant was not seen	k_{21}	k_{22}	$k_{2*} = k_{21} + k_{22}$

Figure 6-4. Note how the numbers involved in this example are arranged and how marginal row sums are shown.

Once these four numbers have been computed, a log-likelihood ratio score can be computed to get a raw score.[1, 2] The actual breach score is computed from the raw score by taking the square root and applying a positive sign if $k_{11}/k_1^* > k_{21}/k_2^*$ and applying a negative sign otherwise. A large positive value indicates that consumers have transacted with the merchant in question disproportionately often before fraud was detected.

This breach score is not intended to be a full-scale production model, but it is very effective, especially considering how simple it is.

Results of the Entire System Together

If we connect a breach model to the simulated data, we see that the model is able to identify the compromised merchant from all other merchants very easily. This is exciting, but the real test comes when we apply the test to real data. In Chapter 4, we saw how even with the first iteration of the data generator and without close matching of a number of the performance indicators—such as the number of merchants or average number of transactions per user—the performance signature of the breach model applied to this simulation was

---

1 The Wikipedia page on the G test (*https://en.wikipedia.org/wiki/G-test*)

2 Dunning, Ted. "Accurate Methods for the Statistics of Surprise and Coincidence." *Computational Linguistics*, 1993: http://bit.ly/1WSB76Q.

very close to the performance signature of the breach model applied to real data. Refer back to Figure 4-9; it shows the distribution of breach score for the simulated data. One of the largest deviations in performance signatures is that at least one compromised merchant was even more apparent in the real data than in the simulated data.

Figure 4-9 plots the breach score for all merchants and shows that the breached merchant has a score that is far above other merchants. This result indicates that this particular breach model is very good at finding the compromised merchant. The graph shows data binned by score with the number of merchants in the bin on the x-axis and the mean score for the bin on the y-axis. For the compromised merchant, only one merchant is in the bin, so the mean is the actual score.

Handy Tricks

Log-synth provides a number of samplers for distributions that are not well known but that are very useful for generating realistic transactional data for the `CommonPointOfCompromise` sampler. One of the most important is the `ChineseRestaurant` sampler. The `ChineseRestaurant` samples integers from a long-tailed distribution where some values are much more common than others and many values occur only once. The total number of unique values you see from such a sampler increases without bound as you take more and more samples, but the rate of growth is a fractional power (like a cube or square root) of the number of samples.

In the common point of compromise simulation, the `ChineseRestaurant` sampler is used to pick merchant IDs for transactions. The parameters used in the common point of compromise simulation mean that the number of unique merchants seen so far will be very roughly $100 \times n^{0.3}$, where n is the number of transactions seen so far.

When dealing with stateful transactional data as described in this chapter, it is very nice to be able to generate an entire history for a single user before proceeding to the next user. This saves memory, but it also allows us to generate data in parallel because the history of one user is independent of other users. To reflect this structure and simplify the way that data is handled in log-synth, it is very elegant to be able to pass around values as JavaScript objects. This elegance translates into code simplicity, but it also means that the resulting data is not in a pure relational form when it comes out of log-synth. Instead, what we will see are JSON objects with user info and an array of complex objects representing transactions.

With the right tools, however, the fact that log-synth produces nested data is actually an advantage because it allows us to hide details and easily handle many complex cases. Apache Drill is one tool that is particularly apt at processing such nested data. As an example, we can count the total number of transactions we have seen as well as the number of unique merchants seen with this query:

```
with basic_stat as (
  select * from dfs synth.`simdata.json`),
flat as (
  select id, flatten(history) as tr from basic_stat),
transactions as (
  select id user_id, flat.tr.merchant merchant,
         flat.tr.`timestamp` ts, flat.tr.fraud fraud,
         flat.tr.`date` date_time from flat)

select count(1), count(distinct merchant)
from transactions;
```

In this query, we have three progressively refined table expressions: basic_stat, which is the original data from log-synth; flat, which is a relational form of basic_stat; and transactions, which has the same relational form as flat, but with the data unnested and labeled. The final query simply counts records and merchants found in transactions.

Summary

The comparison of simulated and real-world results reported in Chapter 4 for this use case underline the great potential of this way of modeling fraud and merchant compromise as well as the more general usefulness of log-synth and its extensions. One of the key tips for using this method successfully is to only include those performance indices that measure what really matters for your particular example.

The use of Java extensions here also suggests that log-synth may prove valuable for a variety of future use cases as well.

CHAPTER 7

A Detailed Look at log-synth

Log-synth is open source software for generating synthetic data that can mimic the performance of real data, useful especially in situations involving restricted access to sensitive data. This chapter is a detailed technical description of the general purpose and implementation of log-synth, and it should be considered as a how-to guide more than a conceptual discussion. As such, the chapter has some overlap with the technical descriptions of the specific use cases covered in Chapter 5 and Chapter 6 but also goes beyond those examples.

For convenience, here is a link to the Github repository where we make log-synth freely available for your use. This repository also contains pre-packaged samplers and some documentation: *https://github.com/tdunning/log-synth*.

Goals

As a package, log-synth has fairly simple goals:

- Facilitate the creation of realistic random data by non-specialists
- Be fast enough to generate big data–scale datasets quickly
- Allow schemas to be defined that combine various building blocks flexibly
- Make it easy to extend log-synth with new samplers

- Keep the system and the user experience really simple

In order to meet these goals, log-synth has been designed with a minimalist point of view in terms of overhead and structure, but with a very generous attitude toward the variety of built-in samplers. These goals have meant that while log-synth contains a wide variety of primitive generators for things like names, addresses, ZIP codes, and vehicle identification numbers, no provision is made for post-processing of data or for scripting the generation of data. The thought is that these complex capabilities can be better added using external tools.

So far, log-synth has met all of the goals set forth originally. It has proved reliable enough to use in real situations, although, by nature, it is the sort of tool that does not tend to be used in production. Instead, it's typically used in testing, model development, or bug fixes.

There is no pretense that log-synth is the only way to generate random data. There are many other methods that are probably better for many situations. We will provide pointers to some of those tools in the last part of this chapter. However, *when you need a simple, flexible, effective, and fast tool for generating useful synthetic data, there is a very good chance that log-synth is what you need*, or nearly so. This observation is particularly applicable if you need to generate synthetic data using performance-signature matching as the figure of merit for the generated data.

Maintaining Simplicity: The Role of JSON in log-synth

The log-synth system uses the JSON data model internally. Note that this is not the same as using the JSON data format, but is a way to manipulate general data structures. JSON is a row-oriented complex data format with the convenience of having a standardized, human-readable format. JSON data is often nested.

The schema that controls generation of data by log-synth is expressed in JSON. The samplers that actually generate the data are constructed based on JSON specifications. Even the random data generated by log-synth is generated and manipulated in memory as JSON data objects. The use of a uniform and flexible data abstraction such as JSON has many benefits, but the most important is the simplicity of the core structure of log-synth. That simplicity makes it easy to understand and extend log-synth.

An interesting side effect of the uniform use of JSON data to represent log-synth schemas is the way that anywhere a sampler would normally accept a value, say as a parameter, it can now accept a JSON specification of a sampler. This makes it very easy to build samplers that generate sequences of, well, anything. It also opens the door to important long-tailed distributions.

It is a conscious design decision for log-synth not to support generalized post-processing or the injection of a scripting language such as JavaScript into the specification of data generators. Similarly, a single schema in log-synth can only generate a single dataset. The rationale for these decisions was that the benefit would be very small since tools such as Apache Drill can directly process the JSON data produced by log-synth. In addition, log-synth can be programmed very easily from a Java program in any case.

Integration with scripting languages such as JavaScript (via Nashorn) or Python (via Jython) would be relatively easy, but that integration is not currently supported.

Log-synth also does not support probabilistic programming or Markov Chain Monte Carlo (MCMC) sampling. This was done partly to maintain the simplicity of log-synth, but also because probabilistic programming and MCMC methods are tricky to use at the best of times, and can be extraordinarily difficult to parallelize. In contrast, log-synth is easy to understand and use and parallelizes trivially.

Structure

To generate data, log-synth reads a schema that consists of a JSON list of sampler definitions. This schema is used to construct a composite sampler that generates individual records in the form of JSON objects. These records are then written to the output.

Log-synth provides for threading for increased generation performance, on a single machine. Multiple instances of log-synth can be run on different nodes to achieve even high levels of parallelism in data generation.

For the most part, each sampler definition in the schema describes how a single field in the output records will be generated. Such definitions have a consistent form that includes the name of the field and the sampler that should be used to generate the values. Here is a simple example:

```
{
    "name":"random_integers",
    "class": "int"
}
```

This definition will generate integers uniformly distributed between 0 (inclusive) and 100 (exclusive).

Optional parameters can be used to control how the values will be generated. The choices of which parameters can be used depends on which sampler is being used. The integer sampler in the example above allows min, max, format, and skew parameters. The min and max parameters are self-explanatory. The format parameter allows integers to be generated as strings in different formats, such as in hexadecimal or with zero padding. The skew parameter allows the integers to be sampled predominately from the smaller values in the allowable range (for positive skew) or the larger values (for negative skew).

Sampling Complex Values

Many samplers produce complex objects instead of simple numerical or string values. For instance, the zip sampler generates ZIP codes, but it packages another 11 fields of information along with the basic ZIP code itself. These additional fields include the city and state for the ZIP code as well as census-derived information (for some ZIP codes), such as the number of income tax–reporting households and total income. Other data has to do specifically with the status and type of the ZIP code, such as whether it refers to P.O. boxes or business addresses.

Another example of a sampler that produces complex output is the vehicle identification number (vin) sampler. The fields that the VIN sampler produces vary by the type of car, but the year and make are typically included. For some manufacturers such as BMW or Ford, the sampler can include information on engine type or where the plant that is supposed to have assembled the vehicle is located.

Most of the samplers with complex outputs allow you to limit the fields to be included in the output (using a fields parameter) and may even allow you to limit the output to a simple string (by setting the `verbose` parameter to `false`).

These complex samplers also often let you limit the output to only include records that satisfy certain constraints. ZIP codes can be limited to only those that appear, say, within 200 miles of the heart of Los Angeles by using this specification:

```
{
    "name": "zLosAngeles",
    "class": "zip",
    "near": "34.02,-118.41",
    "milesFrom": 200
}
```

Similarly, you can generate VINs only for vehicles assembled by Ford in North-America (i.e., in the US, Canada, and Mexico) in the 1990s by using this specification:

```
{
    "name": "fordsFromAmurrica",
    "class": "vin",
    "country": "north_america",
    "make": "ford"
    "years": "1990-1999"
}
```

Structuring and De-structuring Samplers

Having data that is nested like that generated by the `vin`, `zip`, `ssn`, and other samplers is fine if the output is JSON data, but it can be problematic if the consumer of the data needs data in a format that doesn't support nested data, such as comma separated (CSV) data. Log-synth has a sampler called `flatten` that gets rid of a layer of structure to help solve this problem. For instance, if we want to have the city, state, and ZIP code fields from the `zip` sampler as fields in a record, we could use this specification:

```
{
    "class":"flatten",
    "value": {
    "class": "zip"
        "fields":"city,state,zip"
    }
}
```

Note that neither the flatten nor the zip samplers have names. That is because the names are supplied by the fields that are in the values the zip sampler produces.

Contrarily, in some cases we want more structuring rather than less. For instance, we might generate a customer's name and address and then want to sample a variable number of transaction times for that same customer. In that case, we could use the sequence sampler to sample from an underlying sampler multiple times, putting the results into a list. The map and join samplers perform similarly with different result structures.

Finally, we might want to pick randomly from any number of samplers and sample from one of them chosen at random. This can be done using the mixture sampler.

As an example, this specification samples ZIP codes that are within 53 miles of New York, or San Francisco, but it completely ignores the center of the US:

```
{
    "class":"mix",
    "rates":[2, 8],
    "values": [
        {
            "class": "zip",
            "fields":"city,state,zip",
            "near": "40.7033127,-73.979681",
            "milesFrom": 53
        },
        {

            "class": "zip",
            "fields":"city,state,zip",
            "near": "37.7577,-122.4376",
            "milesFrom": 53
        }
    ]
}
```

Flattening and mixing show how higher-order samplers can affect the structure of a result while delegating concerns about the content of the result to other samplers.

Extending log-synth

Extending log-synth is very straightforward if you are familiar with Java programming concepts. The basic idea is that you need to write a new class that extends `FieldSampler`, and you need to tell the `FieldSampler` class about your new class using an annotation in the source of `FieldSampler`. You can follow the example of the existing annotations as a guide.

Once this step is done, you can reference your new sampler in schema definitions using the name that you defined. Any properties in the JSON specification for your sampler will cause setters to be called on your sampler. If you have required properties that must be set, you can define these properties as arguments to your constructor and use a `@JsonProperty("your_parameter_name_here")` annotation (replacing the name, of course) to tell log-synth what the name of the property is.

Currently, all samplers in log-synth have to be defined at compile-time. It is possible that this requirement will be relaxed in the future by providing the ability to specify directories for third-party samplers that log-synth can load at run-time.

Example 7-1 contains an example of a complete sampler that emulates the flipping of a coin. This isn't a particularly important sampler to have, but it shows off the basics of how write a sampler. The initial implementation is always a fair coin with two sides that are labeled "heads" and "tails."

Example 7-1. This class represents just about the simplest possible sampler implementation. This code has a multinomial distribution that will return "heads" or "tails" with equal probability when sampled.

```
public class Coin extends FieldSampler {
    Multinomial<String> names = new Multinomial<>();

    public Coin() {
        names.add("heads", 1);
        names.add("tails", 1);
    }

    @Override
    public JsonNode sample() {
        return new TextNode(names.sample());
    }
}
```

With this definition and after adding an annotation to the `FieldSam pler` class, we can use the following specification:

```
{
    "name":"c1",
    "class":"coin"
}
```

We can extend the Coin sampler by allowing the names and probabilities of the possible sample values to be defined. With this extension, we could have a coin that could land on edge with this
specification:

```
{
    "name":"c1",
    "class":"coin",
    "values": {
        "heads":0.495,
        "tails":0.495,
        "edge":0.01
    }
}
```

To make this work, we only need to add a setter to the Coin class:

```
public void setValues(JsonNode values) {
    names = new Multinomial<>();
    Iterator<String> ix = values.fieldNames();
    while (ix.hasNext()) {
        String option = ix.next();
        names.add(option, values.get(option).asDouble());
    }
}
```

Using log-synth with Apache Drill

Both log-synth and Apache Drill use the JSON data model ubiqui-
tously to structure their internal data (this is not the same as using
the JSON data format externally). This common property means
that there is a fundamental compatibility between them that does
not exist between log-synth and any other SQL-on-Hadoop system.

This fundamental compatibility means that the purposeful limitation on the amount of post-processing that log-synth does is not a
practical issue; if you need complex, logical post-processing and
joining of log-synth data, Drill can very likely help you out.

This is particularly powerful where you need separate tables that
have subtle correlations. Such correlations can be easy to generate if
you generate all of the correlated values in a single record. Drill can
separate those records into the multiple tables where the correla-

tions need to be. Drill can also restructure records on a larger scale than is possible with log-synth–native capabilities such as `flatten`.

In addition, Drill can be used to compute KPIs for your dataset for comparison back to the real data. Because you may want to generate your data in complex forms, say as stateful transaction sequences, computing these KPIs will require a tool that can handle nested data easily.

Finally, Drill is also the simplest way to convert JSON or CSV data into Parquet format. Many applications are beginning to use columnar data formats like Parquet as inputs, so being able to easily convert log-synth output into Parquet is very handy.

Choice of Data Generators

Of course, log-synth isn't the only way to generate random data. There are a large number of other tools that can help with this. The primary reasons to pick log-synth are:

- Easy access to realistic data samplers for things like SSNs, names, and addresses
- Extensibility via Java
- Ability to use output templates
- Ability to write schemas that control the overall synthesis process
- Code is open source

On the other hand, in some situations you may need something different. For instance, if you are working on an algorithm in R, generating your data in R may be better than generating data with log-synth and then loading it into R. You may also need to replicate standard benchmark results, which would require using a generator like the TPCH data generator that is part of a standard benchmark framework. In some cases, you may also need more advanced algorithms to sample from your data. That might mean that you should look into a probabilistic programming system like Figaro.

Finally, if you really want to release your original data in a form that can be used to compute certain aggregates, then some of the recent differential privacy preserving systems may be what you need.

Here we examine each of these alternatives and compare them to the log-synth approach.

R is for Random

The R system has a wide variety of probability distributions built in, including, for example, the normal, exponential, Poisson, gamma, and binomial distributions. Each of these distributions includes a function to compute the probability density function and cumulative distribution function and to sample from these distributions. Moreover, R is a general programming language that is highly suited to numerical programming.

All of this means that R may be an excellent choice for generating random data in certain situations. This is particularly true where the desired distribution has complex mathematical structure or depends on having an obscure distribution that has not been added to log-synth. A quick rule of thumb could be that if the distributions mentioned at the beginning of this section are important to you, then R is likely a good choice.

R will be much less appropriate when you need a relational structure, or realistic samples of things like Social Security numbers, ZIP codes, or names, or where the dataset is really large.

Benchmark Systems

A number of benchmarks come with data generators that range from nearly trivial to moderately complex. For instance, the Terasort benchmark that lately has been packaged as the TPCx-HS benchmark generates records with 100 bytes of uniform random bits. This characteristic meets the needs of the TPCx-HS, but it has little utility beyond that one benchmark.

The TPC-H benchmark has a more interesting data generator that builds data from a simple star schema. The benchmark has programs that generate the data at different scales, and this synthetic data is used to test databases in conjunction with 22 queries that make up the benchmark itself.

While the TPC-H data is much more interesting and useful outside of the benchmark itself, the data generator is hard-coded to produce exactly this one dataset with no provision for flexibility. This isn't surprising, since the point of a standardization benchmark is to provide standard data and queries. The schema for the TPC-H benchmark data is shown in Figure 7-1.

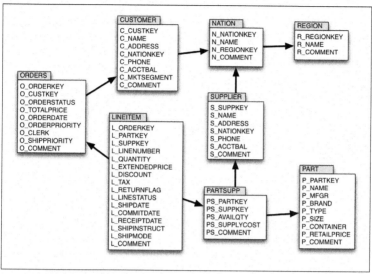

Figure 7-1. The schema of the TPC-H database is fixed in form but scalable in size.

Note that even if you were to modify the TPC-H data generator, it still has no provision for skewed distributions or nested data. This makes it difficult or impossible to reasonably match performance signatures in many cases.

Big data and data warehousing benchmarking didn't end with the TPCx-DS and TPC-H systems, of course. The BigBench benchmark includes a data generator known as DBSynth, which has considerably more flexibility than the TPC-H generator. DBSynth has similar goals as log-synth, but it is not open source, nor is there an open community built around it. DBSynth has more sophistication than log-synth in terms of building data that replicates existing data, but this approach also makes it more difficult to be sure that the models that DBSynth uses are not simply replicating real data in some cases. As such, DBSynth may be less appropriate for sharing data widely.

Probabilistic Programming

The methods used on log-synth are very simple, but they have been observed to work well in some practical situations. There are clearly situations where you might need something fancier, however. As a straightforward example, suppose that you wanted to use the current log-synth to pick 5 ZIP codes for each record such that the ZIP codes are within 20 miles of each other. This specification might be needed to simulate a delivery route, for example.

In the current log-synth, the only easy way to do this without custom programming would be by using something like a rejection algorithm, which samples ZIP codes and tests to see if the results are acceptable. With this particular problem, however, almost all of the samples will be rejected if they are taken uniformly from the set of all ZIP codes.

Probabilistic programming systems are very good at dealing with probability distributions that are constrained somehow. Often, these constraints come from some limited number of observations of a real-world system and are used to let us reason about what is going on under the covers.

As such, probabilistic programming excels when we have a theory that we can express as probabilities, and we want to refine that theory using data we have observed.

The applications in this book, however, are designed to work in a much more pragmatic fashion. Rather than trying to find the truth of the matter, we only try to make data that replicates the key statistics on the output of a model. By narrowing our ambitions so strongly, we gain by having a simpler problem to solve with log-synth. This is not to say that probabilistic programming does not have a useful niche, but rather that we think we can solve a simpler problem using simpler tools and still produce useful results.

Theoretically speaking, the problem of matching the performance signatures the way that we do with log-synth could be posed as just the kinds of constraints that probabilistic programming can work with. Unfortunately, the complex nature of most of the interesting performance indicators is likely to make it hard to use probabilistic programming at all for data sharing, and the performance of any solution is also doubtful.

Differential Privacy Preserving Systems

Another advanced approach to data sharing is based on recent developments in differential privacy preserving systems. These systems add noise to data records and may collapse records together in ways that are mathematically guaranteed to prevent the recovery of individual records.

These systems seem ideal for the data-sharing problem that we talk about in this book. Early systems were limited in the kinds of queries that would return accurate results. More recent systems allow machine learning algorithms applied to the shrouded data to produce useful models that can be applied to the originals.

As such, differential privacy preserving systems seem ideal for data sharing. There are, however, still some substantial problems to solve. The biggest problem is the one of convincing a security review panel to believe that any shrouding or noise-injection problem is going to be sufficient to guard private data. Mathematical proofs of safety are designed to convince mathematicians and are often much less convincing to non-mathematicians. When dealing with security, there is always the suspicion that such a proof was based on idealizations of how things work, rather than on the far less-than-ideal world of real data and fallible humans. Even worse, guarantees of differential privacy are made in these proofs in probabilistic terms, while security requirements are typically couched in absolutes—"probably won't leak" is different from "will not leak." That also makes it hard to sell these approaches.

A secondary issue is that it is not clear whether machine learning applied to shrouded data will work the same as it does on the original data. The noise injected to shroud the personal data can make the learning process behave very differently than on the original data.

The landscape is changing with regard to differential privacy methods, but for now we view log-synth and performance signature matching a much simpler approach and one much more likely to be implemented correctly, particularly because the only data transferred out of the security perimeter is small and inspectable.

Future Directions for log-synth

The experience so far with log-synth has led to many improvements and extensions. Working with financial institutions has led to many samplers that can be used to emulate transactions and fraud. Working with manufacturers has led to samplers that help emulate industrial processes. Working with logistics companies has led to samplers that can emulate trucks on the road.

But even with as many samplers as log-synth already has, there are many more yet to be built. Wouldn't it be interesting to have emulators for ship voyages? (Yes, according to one company.) What about the ability to sample IP addresses and generate packet-capture logs? (Yes, according to a large networking company.)

What else would be interesting in your applications? Obviously, only you can say. Log-synth is an open project, however, and contributions and comments are very welcome.

To make contributing easier, one likely improvement for log-synth in the near future would be to add the ability for developers to publish samplers in a form that allows users to download and use these samplers quickly and easily.

Another ease-of-use improvement that is likely in the future is the ability to treat a log-synth schema as if it were a virtual table. With this capability, log-synth would be considered an input source for a system like Apache Drill, and you would be able to query random data directly without having to pre-generate data.

Performance of systems using random data is also very important. To facilitate this, adding the ability to output data in Parquet format instead of JSON or CSV formats is being considered.

CHAPTER 8

Sharing Data Safely: Practical Lessons

This book has looked at the flipside of security: how to safely use or share sensitive data rather than how to lock it away.

The benefit of working with big data is no longer a promise of the future—it's become an increasingly mainstream goal for a wide variety of organizations. People in many sectors are already making this promise a reality, and as a result, it is increasingly important to pursue the best practices for keeping data safe.

Data at scale is a powerful asset, not only for business strategies but also for protection. Collecting and persisting large amounts of behavioral data or sensor data provides the necessary background to understand normal patterns of events such that you can recognize threatening or anomalous occurrences. These approaches provide protection against financial attacks, terrorist attacks, environmental hazards, or medical problems. In big industrial settings, saving years' worth of maintenance records and digging into them in combination with streams of sensor data can provide predictive alerts for proactive maintenance that avoids expensive and sometimes dangerous equipment failures. These examples make it clear that saving and using big data is a huge advantage. The question is how best to do this safely.

We started with the analogy of buried treasure known as the Cheapside Hoard, hidden so well that it remained unclaimed for almost 300 years. The lesson to be learned for modern life that embraces big data is that, while it's important to build a secure system, it's also useful to ask yourself: can you lock down data without making it so secure it's lost to use?

In Chapter 2, we recounted stories of problems encountered when people shared sensitive data publicly. These stories were not provided to make you be fearful, but rather to alert you to potential risks so that you will avoid similar problems while working with your large-scale data. The trick is to learn practical methods to help you manage data access without endangering big data security, whether you plan to publish data, to share it on a need-to-know basis for different internal groups in your organization, or to work with outside advisors without ever having to show them your sensitive data at all.

The main new approaches we suggest include the use of two open source tools for different methods of safe data handling. The first is the open source and open community project, Apache Drill. Drill lets you safely share only as much data as you choose. As a scalable Hadoop and SQL query engine that uses standard SQL syntax, Drill provides the capability to create data views with chained impersonation. Like pieces of a treasure map, Drill views can be defined such that each user or group can see only that subset or variant of data that you want them to see—the remainder of a table stays hidden. Drill views are easy to create and manage, making them a practical approach to safe data use.

The other open source tool we discuss is log-synth, developed and contributed by one of the authors of this book. Log-synth is one of several tools for synthesizing data, but it's a practical choice for use in secure environments in part because of how simple it is to use. One reason to generate fake data for working in a secure environment is to provide the raw material for people outside a security perimeter who are trying to help with query design, bug fixes, model tuning, and so on. One of the key lessons we provide is how to tell whether or not the data you've generated is an appropriate stand-in for the real data of interest. Instead of trying to get an exact match for characteristics of the real data, you just need to match the KPIs observed for real or fake data and the process in question. This way of targeting the data you generate makes this method for working safely with secure data particularly easy and therefore practical. You can share the load of working on secure data without ever having to actually share the data itself.

In addition to generating fake data as a substitute for sensitive data in order to work safely with outsiders, log-synth is also useful for producing a smaller, more manageable dataset for experimentation and troubleshooting when down-sampling of relational data is difficult or not appropriate.

Beyond the real-world successes with log-synth that we describe in Chapters 4–6, there are many other use cases in which this approach is proving valuable. Log-synth is open for others to contribute, and it will be even more useful as additional samplers are added.

In closing, we hope that these suggestions will help you access, share, and use the "treasures" that your data holds.

Additional Resources

Many of the following resources were mentioned in the text; others provide additional options for digging deeper into the topics discussed in this book.

Log-synth Open Source Software

Log-synth is open source software that gives you a simple way to generate synthetic data shaped to the needs of your project. It can generate a wide variety of kinds of data and it's fast and very flexible.

Please note that not only is log-synth open source, but it is open community as well—contributions are very welcome.

- **Log-synth on Github:** Site includes software with various pre-packaged samplers, extensions related to the fraud detection use case, and documentation. *http://bit.ly/tdunning-log-synth*

- **Sample code for this book on Github:** *Sharing Data Safely: Managing Big Data Security*, Chapters 5 and 6. *http://bit.ly/log-synth-share-data*

  Site includes the source code for the example from Chapter 5 about building sample relational data. Also included is source code that shows how to generate and analyze data for the single point of compromise fraud model described in Chapter 6.

- **"Realistic Fake Data" whiteboard walkthrough video by Ted Dunning:** *https://www.mapr.com/log-synth*

Apache Drill and Drill SQL Views

Apache Drill is an open source, open community Apache project that provides a highly scalable, highly flexible SQL query engine for data stored in Apache Hadoop distributions, MongoDB, Apache HBase, MapR-DB, and more.

You're invited to get active in the community via project mailing lists, meet-ups, or social media.

- **Apache Drill project website:** *https://drill.apache.org/*
- **Follow on Twitter @ApacheDrill:** *https://twitter.com/apache drill*
- **Free resources for Apache Drill via MapR:** Includes free online Drill training, white papers, presentations, and download for Drill tutorial/sandbox. *http://bit.ly/mapr-drill-resources*
- **Apache Drill documentation on Views:**
  — Create view command: *http://bit.ly/apache-drill-view-create*
  — Browse data using views: *http://bit.ly/apache-drill-views-browse*
- SQL Views discussed in Chapter 14 of *Learning SQL, 2nd edition* by Alan Beaulieu (O'Reilly , 2009)

General Resources and References

Cheapside Hoard and Treasures

- Fosyth, Hazel. *Cheapside Hoard: London's Lost Treasures: The Cheapside Hoard* (*http://bit.ly/cheapside-hoard-bk*). London: Philip Wilson Publishers, 2013.
- Museum of London (*http://bit.ly/1i1IjO1*)

Codes and Cipher

- Civil War Code (*http://nyti.ms/1Jy3Bx1*)
- Vigenére Cipher (*http://bit.ly/1gXTHJG*)

Netflix Prize

- Contest website (*http://bit.ly/netflix-prize-1*)
- Netflix prize leaderboard (*http://bit.ly/netflix-prize-leader*)
- Narayanaan, Arvind and Vitaly Shmatikov. "Robust De-anonymization of Large Datasets (How to Break Anonymity of the Netflix Prize Dataset)." February 5, 2008. PDF (*http://bit.ly/de-anonym-pdf*).

Problems with Data Sharing

- "Musings on Data Security" blog on poorly masked card account numbers (*http://bit.ly/card-digits*).
- Goodin, Dan. "Poorly anonymized logs reveal NYC cab driver's detailed whereabouts." *Ars Technica*, 23 June 2014: *http://bit.ly/nyc-taxi-data*.

Additional O'Reilly Books by Dunning and Friedman

We have written these other short books published by O'Reilly that you may find interesting:

- *Practical Machine Learning: Innovations in Recommendation* (February 2014): *http://oreil.ly/1qt7riC*
- *Practical Machine Learning: A New Look at Anomaly Detection* (June 2014): *http://bit.ly/anomaly_detection*
- *Time Series Databases: New Ways to Store and Access Data* (October 2014): *http://oreil.ly/1ulZnOf*
- *Real-World Hadoop* (March 2015): *http://oreil.ly/1U4U2fN*

About the Authors

Ted Dunning is Chief Applications Architect at MapR Technologies and active in the open source community.

He currently serves as VP for Incubator at the Apache Foundation, as a champion and mentor for a large number of projects, and as committer and PMC member of the Apache ZooKeeper and Drill projects. He developed the t-digest algorithm used to estimate extreme quantiles. T-digest has been adopted by several open source projects. He also developed the open source log-synth project described in this book.

Ted was the chief architect behind the MusicMatch (now Yahoo Music) and Veoh recommendation systems, built fraud-detection systems for ID Analytics (LifeLock), and has issued 24 patents to date. Ted has a PhD in computing science from University of Sheffield. When he's not doing data science, he plays guitar and mandolin. Ted is on Twitter as *@ted_dunning*.

Ellen Friedman is a solutions consultant and well-known speaker and author, currently writing mainly about big data topics. She is a committer for the Apache Drill and Apache Mahout projects. With a PhD in Biochemistry, she has years of experience as a research scientist and has written about a variety of technical topics, including molecular biology, nontraditional inheritance, and oceanography. Ellen is also co-author of a book of magic-themed cartoons, *A Rabbit Under the Hat*. Ellen is on Twitter as *@Ellen_Friedman*.